PLAYING AMONG THE STARS:
SHOOTING BALLS OF LIGHT AND LOVE FROM

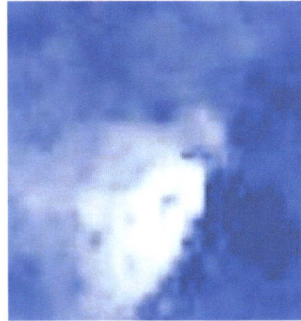

THE OPEN VEIL

DIARY OF SPIRITUAL EXPERIENCES WITH PHOTOS FROM SPIRIT

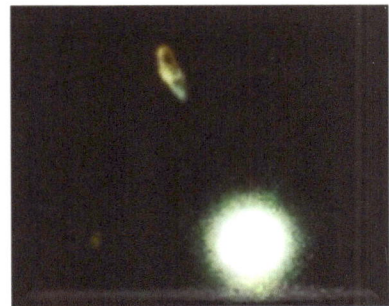

ZoeLouise CadeJacobs

COPYRIGHT PAGE

ISBN # 10 – 0-692-79588-X
ISBN # 13 – 978-0-692-79588-0

PUBLISHER@M. LOUISE JACOBS
ljacobscade199@gmail.com

DEDICATION

DEDICATED TO MY CHILDREN, SPOUSES (WHICH I CONSIDER MY CHILDREN) AND GRANDCHILDREN

STEVEN, SANDI, MADISON
RACHAEL, TONY, GABRIEL, JACOB
CADE, LAURA, CAITLYN, PETER
FAITH, RYAN, EDWARD, LUKE

MY 'MAMA' AND 'DADDY'
Brothers and their families; In-laws; Grandparents; Aunt; Uncles; Cousins
MY GREATEST TEACHERS AND GUIDES (ANGELS): Zoe, Lizzie, Black Beauty, Jake, Sammy, Cleo, Skippy, Maggie (all 7 puppies), Trigger
ALL OF NATURE
FRIENDS THAT WALKED WITH ME ALONG MY PATH:
Debbie W; Claire G; Mary C; Suzanne J; Vernice V; Irma T; Charles D; Judy B; Suzanne B; Rosie D; Barbara C; Robert C; William B; Stan N; Karen & Barney C; Bro Jerry & MS Virginia; Sandra S.W; Jamie L; Jay & Lissette T; Bonnie G; Brenda B; Carol T; Sandra L; Adam H; Meghan C. & Fur Babies.
All my many 'STUDENTS' that shared my journey in life.
A SPECIAL' THANK YOU' TO: Millie and Charles (Chuck) M.
Charles (Chuck), Ann & Bianca B.
Don & Ginny F.
Terry S.
Jackie H.
Phyllis T. G.

TABLE OF CONTENTS

INTRODUCTION

My unending search for truths in life enabled me to write my book. I consider my work more of a 'documenting of my experiences' rather than a true writing experience. My experiences support the belief that we are connected and our love with our departed loved ones is eternal. The experiences also support the belief our relationship with our beloved animal companion is eternal. My experiences support the fact that consciousness does exist outside our physical body and we are able to connect with all God's beings after their passing into new life.

It took me most of my earthly life to become aware of the love, guidance and teachings given to me from our spirit world that surrounds us. My angels and guides, which include my passed over' fur 'babies and relatives, are there to assist me on my journey. I was always aware they were there, but did not know how to utilize their assistance with my challenges faced in life. I now realize my true self is a beautiful and powerful spirit. I also realize I have never been alone in life.

At times my life became burdened from the harsh drama filled earth reality. I learned to bring into cooperation my challenged reality and my inner truths and power. I began to realize if I made decisions based upon others' beliefs and society in general, I would spin 'out of control' quickly. When I received messages from my soul to go within for truths and guidance, I was naive as to the method. Through many trials, I learned how to quiet my surroundings and open up to the reality of the 'open veil'. The love I found is astounding and left me many gifts.

This little book is a means of documenting my spiritual experiences. It is my hope it will be read and passed down as a tool of spiritual guidance within my family. It is also a gift from spirit for all animal lovers. My animal companions, along with my human family, helped me with my grieving process along my path in life. God allowed me a glimpse into the veil ensuring the peace I sought when they passed. God is love and lives within all beings. Love is eternal and we are all connected.

EXPERIENCE # 1

My spiritual self is my true self and always present within. This memoir is documenting the times my physical self was able to peek into the 'other side of the veil'. It is only a memoir in that I am pulling out my spiritual experiences as documentation. It is not a writing of my life's journey. The book includes the' spiritual photos' sent to me along my path. This little book also includes several photos of my journey.

My soul's growth moved my physical body from a naive southern belle to a young military solider. My growth continued with lessons learned in the following roles: wife; Mother; high school teacher; divorced woman; single parent; Mother to 7 kitties and many strays; Grandmother; retiree; hospice volunteer and finally, a new writer. My reality has always been intertwined with visits from and to our Heaven (Afterlife).

My earthly journey began on a farm in Mississippi. Along with my Mother (we called her Mama) and Daddy, I had two younger brothers. I was blessed to be part of a large extended family unit. My Mother's family consisted of 10 siblings. My Dad's family, consisted of 6 siblings. We were never alone as children, for we had a large number of 'cousins'. There were 31 first cousins on one side of the family and 16 on the other side of the family. I was blessed to be raised in close proximity to my grandparents. It was a blessing having the families close enough to visit often in life. The families were bound by a' great love of family and faith'.

I feel my awakening to my spiritual journey began at the age of two years. As a young teen, my Mother explained the illness I encountered at a young age in life. She explained I was critically ill with double pneumonia. Days later, my kidneys began to shut down. She stayed at my side in the hospital for fourteen days and nights praying for a miracle. My fever was very high and my body was packed in ice. The doctor informed my parents I had approximately two hours to live. She showed me the scar of which I still carry, on my left ankle. My veins were so weak, they had to cut an incision in order to give me blood transfusions. One of my uncles gave me blood. The family kept the 'Faith'; they all surrounded me with prayer. My fever soon broke and my body began to function again. I am grateful I survived and was able to continue my journey in life.

Documenting my experiences is my story from my perspective as I walked along my path in life. I truly believe we plan this earthly journey along with our God, Angels and Guides. In so doing, I chose to live the beginnings of my life in that particular time period in that state in that family to learn many lessons for myself and my family. I know my family to be truly good and loving human beings. I am able to understand their perspectives of life. They knew I felt a conflict inside that pushed me forward with my search for knowledge of truths in life. I knew my family to be truly proud and patriotic people living in a slow to change state that was in conflict. I was proud to be from Mississippi, but could not understand the toxic conflict of the era in which I grew up. I had concerns for what I questioned as injustices. I was highly sensitive to the lives of all beings.

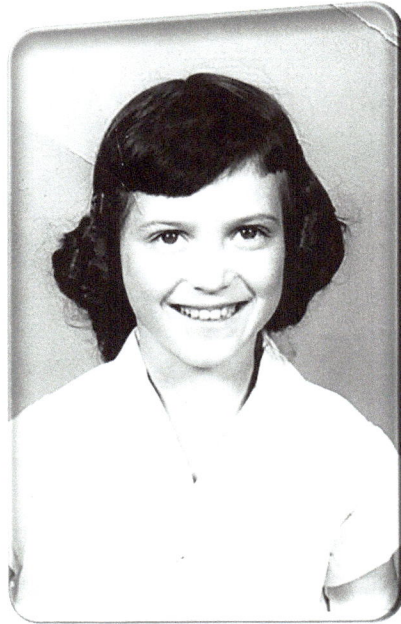

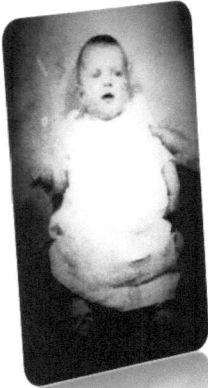

EXPERIENCE # 2

I endured a long and hard delivery with my first child, Steven, Jr. I was transferred to the surgery floor following delivery. During the surgery, I experienced my first 'out of body experience'. I awoke to a beautiful bright loving light. I have encountered that loving light many times since along my path.

I was totally at peace just floating around the room. I remember looking down from above and seeing the surgeons working on my body. I could see them in blue gowns and masks and hear them talking. Soon, I heard one of them yell out, 'she is awake'! I never felt any pain. I only felt love and happiness.

At the time, I did not realize the importance of such an event. I did not inquire as to what actually happened to me during surgery. My doctor did say he felt I would not want to have any more children due to my first child birth experience in life.

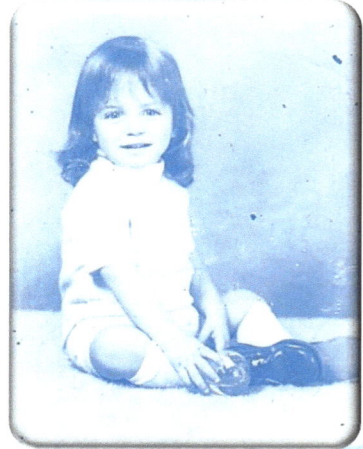

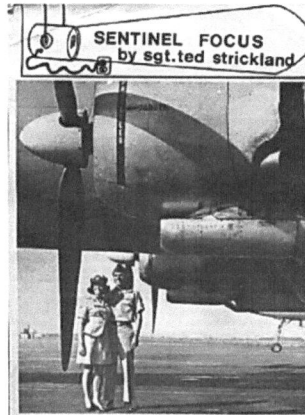

SERGEANTS LOUISE AND STEVEN JACOBS

A family and a home somewhere in New York state are the eventual hopes of Sergeant Louise Jacobs, one of the six members of the Women's Air Force assigned to the 552nd Airborne Early Warning and Control Wing.

Sergeant Jacobs works in the Chief of Administrative Services office as a clerk and has been assigned to McClellan AFB along with her husband, Steven, who is a radar operator with the 964th AEW&C Squadron.

Promotions were recently a family affair for Sergeant Jacobs and her husband when they sewed on their Sergeant stripes together last Wednesday.

They met at Keesler AFB, Miss., while they were attending Aircraft Control and Warning Operator Technical School and have been stationed together ever since.

Enlisting in the Air Force in August of 1968, Sergeant Jacobs first went to Lackland AFB, Tex. for Basic Military Training, before being assigned to Keesler AFB, Miss. and Technical School.

Before coming to McClellan AFB in September of 1969,

she and her husband were stationed at Hancock Field, in Syracuse, N.Y. as radar operators assigned to the 4624th Support Squadron, part of the 35th Air Division. She cross trained into the administration career field so that she could accompany her husband to California.

Sergeant Jacobs was born in Macon, Miss. and has attended Noxubee High School in Macon and Mississippi State University at Starkville, where she majored in business for three years.

She was the Reserve Officer Training Corps Sponsor while attending Mississippi State University and was made an honorary Cadet First Lieutenant in the Reserve Officer Training Corps. While at the university, she also sponsored the Rifle Team and went with them to all the shooting meets.

Sergeant Jacobs will leave the Wing for Irakalion, Crete sometime in August and will spend the remainder of her enlistment in the Air Force there.

Along with housework, she enjoys fishing, horseback riding and hunting.

Young Mid-South—

Her Big Aim: Travel Via Milit[a]

By BROOX SLEDGE

NEWSPAPER ARTICLE ON TOP RIGHT: Strickland, T, "SERGEANTS LOUISE AND STEVEN JACOBS', *SENTINEL FOCUS,* USAF, P1, 1970, Print

NEWSPAPER ARTICLE ON BOTTOM MIDDLE: Sledge, B, "Her Big Aim: Travel Via Military", *COMMERCIAL* APPEAL, Memphis, TN, May 1964, Print

35th ADiv Spotlights Amn. Louise Cade

FOLLOWING A TRACK — Amn. Louise Cade uses a light gun to obtain a reading on an aircraft plotted by radar. By using the gun Airman Cade can obtain vital information on the aircraft from computers located within the defense complex. (USAF PHOTO)

NEWSPAPER ARTICLE: NEWS RELEASE, "35th ADiv Spotlights Amn. Louise Cade", USAF, December 21, 1968, p, Print

NEWSPAPER ARTICLE ALSO APPEARED: "Airman Louise Cade Following A Track", *THE MACON BEACON,* January 2, 1969, p 1, Print

MILITARY PHOTO: USAF BASIC TRAINING, August 1968

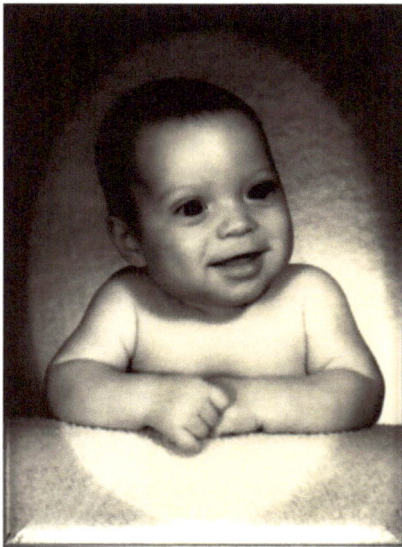

EXPERIENCE # 3

A few weeks prior to the delivery of my third child, Cade, I became aware of my Spiritual Self. My Mother, in her late forties, was in the end stage of a long battle with a cancerous brain tumor. She lived 200 miles away. She suffered greatly for 18 long months. I knew deep in my soul she was holding on awaiting the birth of my son. The entire family lovingly cared for my Mother during her illness. My husband received a job offer in his field a few months prior to my son's birth. I knew I was losing my Mother and in order to move forward in life, we needed to make the move. I knew when my Mother passed, I would be devastated and not be able to relocate my family to a new city. The move would mean I would not see her until after the birth of my son.

I began to hear knocking sounds at night coming from the kitchen cabinets. Finally, I was hearing them from behind my bedroom wall. One night I woke my husband and asked him if he could hear the sounds. He listened for a while, but could not hear the sounds. I called and promised my Mother we would drive down as soon as the baby was born. Deep in my soul, I could feel her concern and distress. She wanted to make sure the baby and I were okay.

Finally, my water broke and I found myself in the hospital ready to have my son. Due to my husband having a new job, his insurance would not cover the birth of the baby. We enrolled into the clinic at St Joseph's Hospital. We were new to the community and did not have anyone to watch our two toddler children. We asked one of our neighbor couples if they could care for the children while my husband took me to the hospital. Leaving MS at the end of my pregnancy meant I would miss my uncle, who was my doctor, delivering our baby. It also meant we would not have family caring for our other children during delivery and my stay at the hospital. Along with Steevie who was three years at the time, we had a daughter, Rachael who was 18 months old. Unfortunately, my clinic doctor found herself stuck in traffic and did not get to the hospital in time to deliver. A new intern delivered our son as his first baby in life.

The policy at the clinic was to administer morphine to the Mother and deliver the baby. I remember the morphine feeling very warm as it went into my veins. I passed out immediately and when I awoke I felt ill and throwing up. I was told our son was born and healthy. Awaiting the nurse to bring in my newborn son, I asked for the phone to call my Mother. I knew she was very spiritual and would know when I went into labor. I told her the baby was born and we were both doing great. When my Aunt answered the phone, she confirmed my Mother had been in distress all day worried about us. I again, told her we would be down as soon as I could get home from the hospital. I was due to stay in the hospital for three days. I did not find out until later from our pediatrician that our baby, Cade, was jaundice and had a broken collar bone from delivery. I am so sorry he came into this world with pain. Getting an intern to deliver was one of the consequences of not having insurance. I was concerned about him performing his circumcision. I was becoming very anxious, for I was not handling my Mother's illness very well in life. My husband could not come to the hospital to visit for he had to take care of our toddlers. I asked the priest to help me get out of the hospital, for I needed to see my Mother. I was able to soon leave the hospital. I called my Mother to tell her we would drive down on Friday after my husband got home from work.

The next morning, a neighbor knocked on my door asking me to 'call home'. He said he received a phone call at his home from my Family with a message for me to please call home. I did not think until much later that my Family did not know his name or number. I called my Mother and reassured her we were coming in two days. She told me she wanted to 'tell me how much she loved me'. My Aunt later told me she remarked, "Louise thinks she will see me on Friday, but I will not be here. I wanted to tell her I love her".

Early the next morning after I laid Cade down from a feeding, I went back to sleep until Steevie and Rachael woke up. Around 8:00 am, I heard a clear and loving male voice in my right ear say, "Honey, I am taking your Mother to Heaven now". I immediately sat up in bed and said, "No, you can't take my Mother". I had no idea who I was talking to. The only male figure I knew in Heaven was my Uncle. He was my Mother's younger brother that recently passed. My Mother still grieved his passing. I will never forget this experience, for it was the first time in my young life I wanted to know all the answers to death. I knew I was on crusade for more answers in my life.

Within hours, my husband came home from work and informed me my Mother entered a coma state at 8:00 am. The doctor said it was time for me to come to the hospital. I called and asked to have my son's pediatrician appointment moved up. It was a very cold November day. The pediatrician did not recommend taking the baby out in the cold for a long trip. He said Cade was still jaundice and has a broken collar bone. I did not even consider not going. I prayed for my son and my Mother. I knew I had to get to my Mother soon. I knew she was suffering and holding on trying to wait for me.

As I looked back at my children in the car, my heart broke for I knew how much they loved her in life. My daughter, Rachael, took her Dad's dark Italian skin coloring. She was very dark and my Mother thought it was beautiful. Rachael had a special connection with her Ganny. My son, Steevie, was a beautiful little hyper boy. No matter what he got into, she just smiled and told him how much she loved him. I could see her teaching my children all about love as she did her own children. She was a great 'teacher of Love' in life. A few years earlier she had told me how much she wanted to be a grandmother like her sister, Hazel, and enjoy her grandchildren.

I remembered her premonition in life. During our middle school years, she called all three children into the living room one afternoon for a chat. She informed us that she would be leaving us at an early age. She said she would be passing to Heaven of cancer. We, as children, did not know what to think. She once told me when she was a little girl, she saw a beautiful woman in a white gown standing at her doorway. She, along all her family, were very religious. During her long illness, she had many encounters with her beloved Jesus. I now realize my Mother was also a very spiritual person in life.

When we arrived at the hospital, we found my cousin and her husband in the waiting room. They took my newborn son and toddlers leading me to my Mother's room. Walking into that room to say goodbye was the hardest memory for me in life. My Uncle and Aunt were with her, along with my Dad and two brothers and their families. I went over and told her I was there with the baby. Even though her body was already cold and she was in a coma, tears began to roll down her cheeks. We all knew she was aware I was with her.

Soon, her heart started to stop and start again. She was still fighting to stay going back and forth for several minutes that seemed like hours. I kept thinking she was in pain, and finally said to myself, 'please, Mama, you can go now'. She stopped trying to come back and passed to her Heaven to be with Jesus. One of the nurses said, "She is gone". I felt empty as they covered her and rolled her away. We gathered my poor Daddy and entered the cold night to go to the farm. It would be the first time I walked into that house without her being the center of our home. Upon entering the house, my young daughter, Rachael, ran back to my Mother's bedroom. She ran out and cried, "Ganny gone"!

I knew nothing of death and kept trying to find her. I could feel her, but did not know how to connect and find her. I was awake most of the night in terrible grief. I asked my soul, "Where is my Mother"? Instantly, I heard loud knocking on the walls. I knew she was somehow with me. She lived 18 long suffering months with nobody to talk to about her dying. She walked her path on her journey with her Jesus. At that time, our society did not prepare us for 'dying with dignity'. We did not have hospice to assist the family in how to deal with the dying. The family did the best they knew how in caring for the family member. I will never forget the family telling me to walk in to see her after her brain tumor surgery and tell her all is well in life. That was so hard for me to do, for the surgeon said she only had approximately three weeks to live. She lay in that bed daily while her physical body deteriorated. Cancer is such an ugly invader to fight. She kept trying to figure out how to make sure all were prepared when she left this earthly life. She did not have anyone willing to openly discuss her passing. Death was notopenly discussed during that time period. It was only mentioned as the person' going to Heaven'. The family kept praying for a miracle. I kept remembering her premonition and wondered how she knew of her upcoming cancer. She was so strong to keep all those feelings inside her soul. I remember her asking people to buy my Dad more coveralls, etc. She even asked if we wanted to stay in the house and live with my Dad. We all talked 'around' the topic of death. She was such a powerful spirit (even on earth) that she was able to arrange for a perfect stranger to knock on my door and give me a last message from her.

Being a hospice volunteer, I often wonder if my Mother had deathbed visions, etc. I am truly sorry I was not able to help either parent with their second most important journey of life, dying. I prefer to reference the process as transitioning to our 'real life'. I now realize those are missed treasured moments. Birth and death represents the 'special moments' of our lifetime. If possible, these moments need to be shared with family. My Mother was very fortunate in having a large and loving family surround her during her lengthy illness. My Aunt was there to assist my Dad when Mother passed out at a red light and rode in the ambulance with her to the hospital in Tupelo. Even though there was not a cure for the deadly cancer, my Uncle, a physician, provided the love, care, medications, etc. needed to assist her daily in her illness. We are blessed to have him as not only our Uncle, but a physician in our family. My Mother's sisters took turns along with the children in caring for my Mother. Her brothers came often for visits. My Dad's family were also there to offer love and support.

I now realize I am more than my physical body and will return home when it fails me in life. It is not a matter of dying, but a mere transition home. The unconditional love Mother taught us will never end. It has been 42 years and I know she has never left me. She has always been there when I needed her and I look forward to my end journey when I will be with her in spirit again. I was young and did not understand what the pastor meant at her funeral when he said, 'she has gone to pave the way for her family'. Now, I truly understand and thank her. I caught a beautiful ray of sunshine pierce through the stain glassed window of the church during the service and knew it was my' Mother'.

EXPERIENCE # 4

I can still see my Dad's hand shaking as he explained his plans for my Mother's grave marker. It was so much harder on him. He was the one that had to stay in that house alone. He would be very lonely living on the farm by himself. He suffered great from the loneliness. I always had problems going back with my Mother gone and can only imagine his pain.

Fortunately, he later married a really good woman, Virginia. My Dad loved my Mother's family enough to ask her parent's permission prior to remarrying. Virginia (Nanny) told me she would never try and take my Mother's place, but would be there if I needed her in life. She loved all the family and was good for my Dad. They were able to attend church; visit family and 'grow old together'. They really took good care of each other.

My fourth child, Faith, was born during our time with Virginia (Nanny). She was so excited about having a baby in the family. She called Faith, 'her little MS America'. The grandchildren called her Nanny. We took the children down and let them stay a week in the summers. They have great memories of their time with them and their cousins. Nanny's health began to fail first with a scare with a cancer. Later, her heart began to give her problems.

She decided to have heart surgery. Even though her daughter thought it was a great idea, my Dad had his reservations about her making it through the surgery. She did not come out of the surgery. Nanny was in the hospital in Meridian fighting for her life for 30 days. My Dad stayed by her side. My brothers and I came for visits on the weekends. I was at my school presenting a fashion show when the call came in that she had passed. I packed for Faith and I to leave the following morning to go to the farm. Around 10 pm, I heard Faith screaming in her crib upstairs. I ran up to her as she was screaming and crying. She was not focusing on me when I first tried to pick her up. She was looking at the ceiling and screaming as loud as possible. I reached down and picked her trying to console her. Suddenly, she stopped screaming out. She opened her eyes focusing on me and cried out in a clear voice, "She said she loves me". I said to her," Nanny came for a visit". I will never forget seeing her in that 'spiritual state'. She understood and did not want to let Nanny go on that night.   Nanny's message to Faith was a great comfort to daddy. On one of our weekend visits with Nanny at the hospital, Daddy took Faith into the ICU for a visit. Even though the nurses said she could not go in, he found a way. Faith found a photo in a magazine years later of a woman in a long white gown. She remarked to me, "It looks like the dress Nanny wore when she came to see me".

 Faith has always been a 'spiritual child'. We were in mass one Sunday and she asked me if I could see the Angels behind the priest. When in elementary school, she came home one day with a big skin on her knee. Faith said, "She told me not to get on that high bar, for I would fall and hurt myself".   During her senior year in high school, she informed her sister, Rachael and I, of a dream she had the previous night. She said she dreamed her ACT scores came in the next day and told us her score. Her sister laughed and remarked, "Sure"! Later in the day, Rachael opened the mailbox and Faith's ACT scores were in the box. Faith was working at Kroger. I was blessed to have all my children work hard early in life. Rachael took the unopened mail to Faith. When she opened the envelope, it was the same score she had dreamed. We were very happy for her. Like most children, as she grew older, she stopped talking about spiritual happenings in her life. I have not discussed such matters with my two boys, but both my girls seem to be very spiritual in nature. Rachael mentioned a few years ago that her Grandmother came by the prior night and they went flying. She thought it was awesome. I realized she probably experienced an out of body experience.

Case produced by my younger brother (BTC) as a 'Tribute/Salute' to our Dad for his service to our great country.

EXPERIENCE # 5

Our family relocated to New York. I sensed something in Dad's voice when I informed him we were moving to New York. Later, a relative informed me of Daddy wondering if he would ever see me again in this life.

It was spring break and I promised Steevie I would drive him to TN for prom at his old school. He would spend a few days with friends while Faith and I visit Daddy. The night before we left, I had my first vivid dream visitation from the spirit world. I know now I often leave my body and visit the spirit realm. I saw my Mother surrounded by a bright white light. She showed herself as being above me to my right. She looked as she did in the last photo taken with my Dad. Her message was short, to the point and very clear. She said she had done well in her last life and would never have to return to the earth world. She said she had been given permission to come and see her children as much as she needed in our lives. She showed me how she would be a little above to observe. She then showed me an open casket. She said it was for my Dad. She disappeared and I sat up in the bed. I reassured myself and said it was only a dream. We were leaving tomorrow to visit my Dad.

We stopped in Virginia after a long day of driving. There were no cell phones at that time. I called home to check on Rachael and Cade. My husband told me I needed to call the Macon hospital. He said my Dad had been in a horrific accident with an 18 wheeler oil truck and the driver was deceased. We repacked the car and began driving. I stopped in Memphis to let my son off at his friend's home.

I entered the hospital early the next morning with my youngest daughter, Faith. When she saw Dad, she began to cry. He was black from all the bleeding and trauma. I could tell he recognized us, for he said, "messed up when hit truck". I was very concerned for he was mostly talking about things in his past. It was a small town hospital and over the years I learned to get second opinions. My two brothers were in the room along with my Uncle and Aunt. My brothers said he had lost a lot of blood and had a bad area from the crash on his back. His head x-ray checked out okay. Besides his confusion, I noticed his leg and foot not moving. I asked to have further tests. With my Uncle and Aunt agreeing, they arranged to move him to a larger hospital for testing. When they went to move him he screamed in horrible pain from his back area. The other hospital informed us he had severe bleeding on his brain and was badly burned on his back. The car had split in the crash and my Dad's back was on the muffler. He did not have a seat belt on and his head hit the roof of the car. It hurts to know my Dad lingered in pain awaiting the proper care from the medical field.

They moved him to a larger hospital in Tupelo, MS. Daddy was visiting the VA in the local town prior to the accident in an attempt to get his benefits increased. Sadly, he was a decorated veteran but did not have enough money to live his life. I remembered a special photo of him standing next to General Douglas MacArthur as they were raising our American flag upon capturing an island during WW II in the South Pacific. The stories reveal he was a scout for the General and had a code name, Lone Wolf. He suffered malaria, was injured and MIA on an island alone for one year of his life. He learned how to cope with hiding from the enemy troops and eating whatever he could find on the island in order to survive. He often told of eating grasshoppers, snakes, etc. The VA in the town obviously did not send his papers through properly. He worked for himself as a builder and farmer and did not have any retirement. He completed the entire process of building from drawing up the house plans to the final inspection for $5.00 an hour. Later in life, my son, Cade, sharing his love for creating and building with my Dad, became an architect. I look at his achievements and think of my Dad. After he passed, one of the relatives informed us he did not want to be a burden to his children. Unfortunately, I always lived away and did not know of the challenges of his daily life. His children loved him and would have helped him with his financial challenges.

He was moved again to a larger hospital for treatment. He was placed in ICU for days. It brought back memories of time spent with my Mother at this hospital. I remembered a family member bringing my toddlers to the side of the hospital in order I could see them during my stay with my Mother. Now, it was my Dad's journey of illness. Our family was still strong and some family member had my young daughter keeping her safe. Dad soon began to have seizures. The doctors explained he was older and they did not know if the swelling in the frontal lobe would go down properly. He was scheduled for burn surgery and moved to a private room.

Days later, my brother and sister-in-law took my Dad's two sisters back to their home town and I moved with Dad to his new room. He was moved to the same floor my Mother's journey took her down. Soon after the nurses left the room, he began to moan and I noticed movement in his forehead.

I saw my Dad look to one side of the end of his bed calling his deceased brother, Bill, and then he turned to the other side of his bed calling his deceased brother, Ed. I could not understand any of the conversation. I asked him what was wrong with him. He turned his head, opened his beautiful sky blue eyes and said, "I am going to Heaven to be with your Mother now". Again in life, I reacted out of fear of someone I love dying. I reacted in a manner that displayed how little I knew of death. I said, "No Daddy, you are okay. You are not dying. They just moved you from ICU to your own room". He looked back at the corner of his bed and then said to me, "You do not understand what it is going to be like for me". He closed his eyes and began to moan and move his forehead again. I pushed the button for the nurses.

I really thought I was learning, but when I look back at my response to my Dad, I did not know anything about the dying process and how to be of assistance.

I am the only one that got to hear him speak clearly after the accident. It was spiritual intervention. He loved me enough to be my teacher and stay. He was told the consequences of hard and long suffering and given the choice of exit then or later. I was wrong, for he never got better. He had a long and suffering two year journey prior to passing into his Heaven.

He went from a scary nursing home stay to a lonely VA ward. Faith and I drove down at times for a visit. Even though she was young, the hospital staff always allowed us to visit Dad. Once, I found him very neglected in the nursing home. Faith and I weathered a storm once and found him in a bed with 9 stitches in his forehead from falling out of the bed in the VA hospital. Another time we took him for a ride in a wheelchair to the lobby. When we were rolling him back and he saw the hall going to his room, he looked back at me and began to yell, "No, No". To recall breaks my heart. Like my Mother, we loved our Daddy very much in life. Both parents suffered long illnesses prior to passing. We tried to help the best we knew how. We were young adults busily working taking care of our families. One of my brother's lived close to my Dad. He, his wife and son did all they could to visit and care for him and his place.

In the end, he was in the last bed on an 'old ward'. I remember going over and opening the dusty, tattered shade on the window to allow some light in the room. He was hooked up to tubes and instruments. He looked towards me with those blue eyes and turned to the instruments. I still knew little, but I realized he wanted to 'let go'. I was beginning to slowly learn. I spent the night on the couch in the little waiting room across the hall. The next morning I called a cab to pick me up for the train station. I sensed his time was close. A team of doctors and interns entered the room as I was saying' goodbye'. I saw them sticking him and drawing blood. I noticed him twitch in pain from the sticks. The doctor made a comment about his heart' still being strong'. I stopped at the nurse station and requested a Chaplin for my Dad. I did not think he had much time left in this world. It was heartbreaking to know he spent the last two years of his life either strapped to a wheelchair or bed. He was a hyper man full of energy living an active life prior to the accident. In the end, he lived the life of 'a lone wolf'. Hopefully, he learned how to go within himself and know he was 'never alone'.

I left on Easter Sunday to return to New York. A few days later, I received a phone call. When I answered, I could only hear a distant voice. I could not understand the message. Soon, the phone rang again and it was my brother with the news of my Daddy's passing.

As a hospice volunteer, I took the eleventh hour training. After my Dad passed' alone' on the hospital ward, I wanted to be of assistance when a patient does not have family with them at the end of life. Of course, I believe when our spirit leaves our physical body, our spiritual family are there along with our Angels and Guides to help us transition.

NEWSPAPER ARTICLE ON RIGHT: "Brothers Meet In South Pacific", *THE MERIDIAN STAR,* Meridian, MS, December 2016, Print

Remembering Christmases past

• • • • •

Brooksville brothers reunited during World War II

BY JOHN D. BROMMER SR.

Somewhere in the Phillipine Islands ... December 1943

"Hey, Cade, there's someone you gonna want to see coming down his way tonight," the mail clerk called out cheerfully to Sgt. Bill Cade, who was hunched down over a cup of thick, bitter coffee in the thick, bitter part of a war. The war was so foreign in all ways to this young Brooksville, Miss. farm boy who had been thrust into being a man, and a fighting man at that.

Thousands of miles from home on an island, fighting the Japanese, he was with men from all parts of America. Cade looked up at the mail clerk, but couldn't begin to guess who he had meant. He was pretty sure it wasn't Betty Grable.

Later that evening, Cade saw the silhouette of a jeep against the Asian sky with a passenger bobbing up and down as the driver leaned left and right to control the jeep on an uneven trail. Sgt. Cade's eyes were young and sharp, but the jeep swerved close by as the passenger rose to jump before they came to a full stop. Sgt. Bill Cade, of the 51st Fighter Group of the Army Air Forces, recognized something familiar before he came face to face with Private Sam Cade of the 31st Division of the Army. The two brothers, so far from their roots in Mississippi, were totally unaware they were in the same part of the world, and embraced unashamedly.

"Hot damn, it's you, Sam!" Bill said through a wide grin as tears ran down both men's cheeks, not long before covered with the peach fuzz of youth. They wept, hooped and hollered as loud as they dared with the Japanese always close by. "Yep, and you, Bill!" replied Sam. They rejoiced that from separate units, even separate branches of the service, they were joined for a time serendipitously in God's providence.

In spite of the constant imminence of danger, and the sporadic fighting against the fanatic Japanese, both of the brothers' commanding officers granted them a day to be together for this strange and foreign Christmas.

The hour of separation came too soon, as it is prone to do. They hugged their goodbyes, acknowledging verbally they might never see each other again.

A Christmas miracle in a forbidding jungle about two brothers from the South; a part of what has recently become known as "the greatest generation." This one with a happy ending, in that Bill and Sam made it home to Brooksville, Miss. ... never the same, of course, and never again to be boys."

Sgt. Bill and Sam Cade parents were Wallace and Maggie Cade of Brooksville. Both boys are now deceased as well as their parents. Their two sisters are Margaret Redus of Crawford and Mildred Randall of Brooksville.

THE NEWSPAPER ARTICLE: Brommer, SR, John D., "Remembering Christmases Past", *THE BEACON,* Macon, MS, December 24, 2015, p 15, Print

During the documenting of my experiences, I began to focus upon one of my experiences.   I will write of it later in my little book. The experience lead to the title of my memoir of experiences. I longed for a photo of the beautiful night sky I saw during my experience.   I began to look at the night sky for a few days. Finally one evening as I turned off the lights for bed, I saw an ORB outside my bedroom window (June 21, 2016). I noticed many orbs in the sky. I used my phone camera to capture these amazing photos. The one close to my bedroom window stayed with me all night. One photo reflects it on my upper curtain.   It was still there when daylight arrived. Until that morning, I did not realize you could see an orb in the daylight. I checked later in the morning and they were all gone. They did reappear during the writing of my little book of experiences.   I feel the small one at my window and on my curtain was my beloved kitty, Zoe.

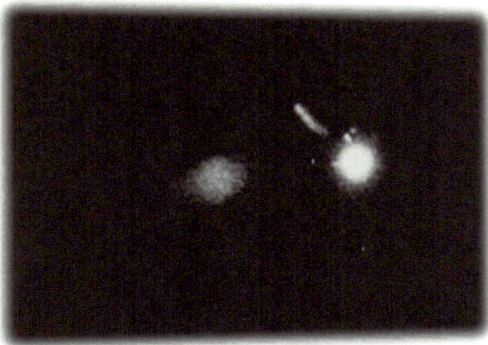

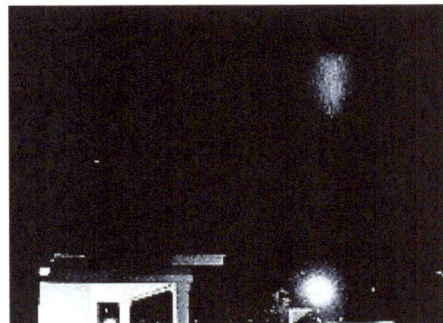

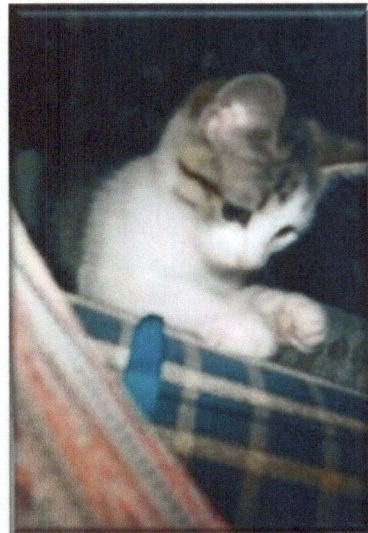

EXPERIENCE # 6

Unfortunately, my journey lead me down a 'path of divorce'. I relocated from New York to Memphis, TN, with my four children. Faith was in elementary school (grade 2) and Cade in high school. Steevie was in college at Syracuse University and Rachael was entering college at Rhodes College in Memphis. Needless to say, I was a very busy single parent working two jobs in life. My daughter's decided to add a new family member. She was my first animal companion and we named her Zoe.

I began to have problems while in New York with cysts in my breasts. My doctor suggested I go to a specialist since one of the cysts was continuing to get larger. The doctor informed me they were sending the fluid from the needle biopsy off for testing. My doctor called in a few days and said the test had reflected some abnormal cells. He gave me the name of a surgeon to consult with about my tests.

The following photos were taken on a teacher trip to Germany in 2008.

I decided to have the lumpectomy on my left breast. I was a single parent with a fear of 'leaving my children alone in life'. I was also working two jobs with little time to worry about my health. I noticed I was beginning to get phone calls with nobody on the line. I previously noticed this happening a few days prior to the passing of a favorite younger cousin. I felt it was a sign from my Mother. During that day, I felt a strong presence touch me with love for a brief moment. It was around the same time my cousin passed. I felt she was saying goodbye to me. As the years have passed, the spirit world has shown me they are very good with electrical equipment as a means to getting messages to us. Many years later, my phone rang many times during the morning with nobody on the line. Later in the day, my youngest daughter had a car accident on her way back to college. Her angels took care of her.

The Sunday afternoon prior to my procedure, I laid down for a little rest. I suddenly went into a meditative trance. The room was filled with bright light. I soon realized I was not alone. First, I saw a spirit come forward. All I could see was a big round ball of light with something inside like a face. At that moment, I saw another and then another. I felt like there were six surrounding my bed. I did not hear any sounds. They were not talking out loud, but I could understand what they were saying to me. One was communicating with the other and they were happy. One told me to look at my body. I looked down and saw a 'really bright green light' surrounding my entire body. I will always remember my fingers all lit up with green light. Their message was, "everything will be okay". Soon, they were gone and I got up to go to the bathroom. As I turned on the light, the switch blew. I reported it to the office. I had so much electricity in my body that it shorted the light.

My oldest daughter drove me to the hospital for the procedure early the next morning. As I left, I asked Cade and Faith to please take our little kitty to the vet, for she was ill. We were a single parent family and only had each other to depend on in life. We always pulled together as a unit.

As I was in the surgery room awaiting the surgeon, one of the team walked in and asked, "Will this be a mastectomy?" I assume he thought I was already out. A nurse informed him they did not know yet. I knew deep down I would be okay. Soon after I awoke, the surgeon called and said the procedure went well. He said he took out all the lymph nodes to be safe, but he did not see anything abnormal. I thanked my God for my healing energy they brought to my tired body on that Sunday afternoon.

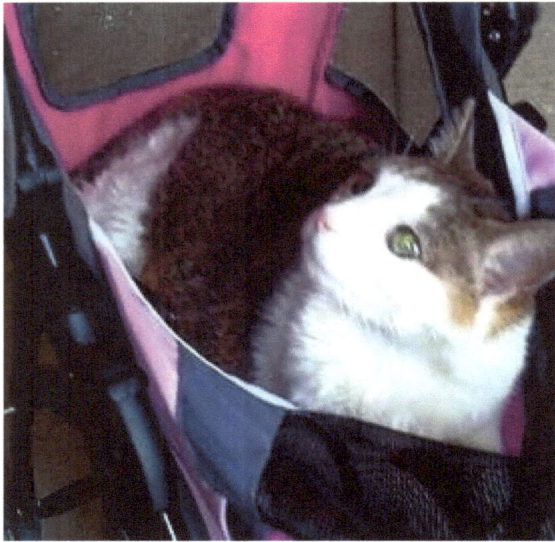

LOVE ALL GOD'S BEINGS

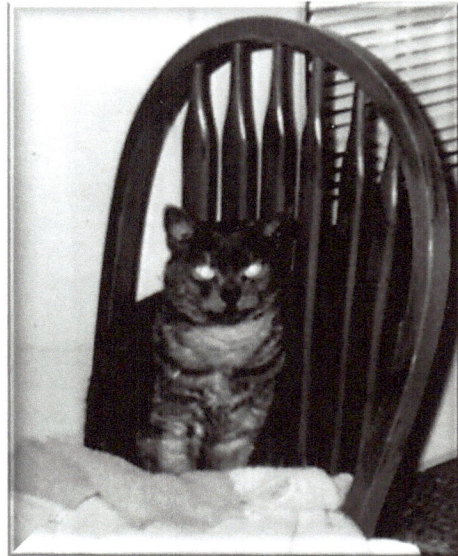

EXPERIENCE # 7

We decided to give Lizzy a home one year after Zoe. I saw one of my students standing on the street in front of Walgreens by my school. She was asking people to give a home to a litter of kittens. Her family could not afford to care for the kittens. I decided to take one to be company to our Zoe. I always wished I had also taken her twin brother, for I hated to separate them in life. We named her Lizzie after my Mother.

It took a few months before Zoe adopted Lizzie, but once she did they were good for each other. Her Mother was white and her Dad black. Therefore, she was white with only the tips of her fur black. She looked a gray color.

I worked so much and the children were in and out of the house. Looking back, I feel sad they spent so much time alone with our busy schedules. Their lives are so short compared to ours. When my life began to slow down, they were already beginning their journey to our heaven.

Lizzie was always thin with lots of energy. They seemed to have different jobs in the house. Zoe was the one that 'guarded' me at night. She always slept at the end of my bed. Lizzie always guarded the front door at night. We could always hear her at night pacing the house with her sounds.

We lived in several apartments, but finally were able to get a home. The kitties loved their home. Lizzie was always the one that met me at the door daily as I entered the home. I treasure the memories I have of them. I would come home from school and feed them. I had

30 minutes to just lay down for a rest before getting back in the car for my night school job. They would lay beside me until I left for my second job and greet me when I came home later in the evening.

Being a school teacher, the students always brought me the strays they found around the school grounds. A few years later, I found a beautiful black cat crying under my car in a dreadful rain. The students and faculty informed me she had been living at the school for many months. She was living in the drain pipes and eating from the dumpster. Nobody seemed to want her and I took her home. Now, we had three animal companions. Rachael named her Black Beauty. She was a Burmese kitty and unfortunately her front claws had been removed prior in life. I wondered how she survived as a stray in the streets with no claws. I assumed she somehow got out of her home and became lost in the impoverished neighborhood. She was constantly looking over her shoulder as she ate her meals. It made Lizzie and Zoe fearful of her when I brought her home. Lizzie and Zoe never seemed to accept her, but they did learn to tolerate her living in the home.

As the years flew by, I spent a lot of my time with my new grandchildren. The kitties learned to love and guard them as our family members. Unfortunately, I became so busy, I did not notice the little signs when they got sick. I remember Rachael remarked to me that Lizzie was losing weight. I had taken her in a few months earlier with a kidney infection. She took her medicine and I assumed she was okay. The vet did not ask me to bring her back in to have it checked. We were living on a very limited income and it was hard to pay for vet services.

Soon, she began to throw up a lot and I could see was ill. I took her with me to school early one morning. I left on my period off and took her to the vet. He called later to tell me her kidney were failing and she needed to be euthanize d. I went into shock. She was only 9 years old. I refused to believe he could not help her. I soon realized I was handling my fur baby's passing as I did my parents. The hardest part was the idea of euthanasia. I could not accept the fact that I was being asked to 'kill my precious little kitty companion". I decided to get a second opinion from another vet. Unfortunately, the second vet turned out to allow her to suffer longer. I was able to bring her home to say goodbye to the other kitties. She stayed overnight at the vets in a big and lonely kennel. When I arrived the next morning he said her breathing was labored with vital organ shutting down. I asked to take her outside for a little while, for she loved to be outdoors. I walked over to the nearby church yard and let her smell the trees and grass.

I cried and begged God to send my Mother to assist in getting Lizzie to Heaven. The younger vet decided to let the older vet euthanize Lizzie. The office was very busy and they put us in a little closet room with an x- ray machine. The older vet came in and told me the procedure. He said he would give her a shot to put her to sleep and later give her the shot to ultimately stop her heart.

As he attempted to administer the shot into Lizzie's thin leg, she looked at the right corner of the ceiling and jumped as high as she could to reach something she saw at the top of the room.

The vet and I looked at each other in amazement. After the shot, he assured me Lizzie was out and he would be back soon to administer the second shot. As soon as the vet closed the door to the little room, Lizzie awoke, sat up, and jumped onto my shoulder. She stared at the wall behind my chair. She opened her mouth and seemed to 'jump' into Heaven. I pulled her down into my arms and closed her eyes. I held her until the vet walked back into the room. He came in ready to administer the shot. I said, "Lizzie is gone"! He said, "What" and grabbed her from my arms. He immediately administered the shot into her chest. I kept yelling that she had passed, for I had witnessed her going. He said he had to put the shot into the heart to make sure she was gone. His technician came to get her in order to take out her IV needle. She brought her back wrapped in her blanket with tears in her eyes. I buried her out in the country at my daughter-in-law's family farm. My son, Steevie, Sandi, and her mother, Patsy helped me bury her body deep into the ground. Lizzie was the first of my animal companions to pass to Heaven (afterlife). She was my first experience at putting them to sleep (euthanasia). It was a cold and emotional event in my life. I understand now that vets are more attuned to hospice care for their animal care at the end. I am so grateful that our society has moved forward in the care and treatment of our animal companions during the end stage of their lives.

I was left puzzled with Lizzie's passing. Most of the people I knew, including religious leaders, believed animals did not have souls and did not pass into our Heaven (afterlife). Our God had allowed me to witness Lizzie as she looked into her Heaven opening her eyes and mouth as she passed. The next afternoon as I sat on my bed crying, I had a split second view of Lizzie walking across my bedroom floor. She walked her same lanky walk. The following Monday morning as I was leaving for school, I saw her materialize again. As I was walking out the door, I looked down at my feet and she was there looking up at me. She quickly vanished from my eyes view. I have seen Lizzie many times since that day appear for brief moments in my life. I truly believe she is one of my guardian angels during this lifetime. In one of my vivid dreams visiting heaven, a woman I was talking to asked me to look down on the floor and see Lizzie. She said, "She will be coming back to you soon". As you will read later in the book, I know she and Zoe are now together.

I am older and look forward to seeing all my 'Fur Babies' when it is my time to 'go home'. I know they mean as much to our God as any human soul and they all pass into our Heaven. I do not believe in a hierarchy of souls. I do believe we have soul growth. As we raise our level of consciousness and vibrations, we will be able to enter into the higher realms. It will also depend upon our desire to move forward. This will lead to more soul growth. The love that connected us on this earth will continue to connect us into eternity.

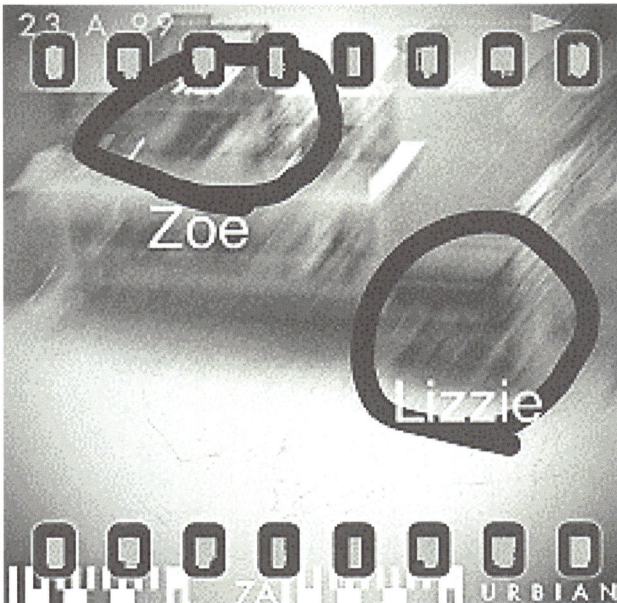

Zoe

Lizzie

(The last two photos are of Zoe and Lizzie after they passed.) ZOE IS LYING ON THE WHITE TABLE. LIZZIE'S DARK GRAY BODY IS LYING ON FLOOR.

EXPERIENCE # 8

I went on a two week TN Teacher Conference to Germany the year prior to my retirement. My daughter, Faith, decided to meet me in Paris prior to returning. It did not take long for me to notice something amidst in our little hotel room.

I entered the small bathroom and placed the toilet items on the shelf. As soon as I left the room, everything on the shelf fell off onto the floor. That evening when I went to shower, the head of the shower began to gush water at a high speed on my head. I pulled my head away and the gushing water from the shower head just moved with me. The water was filling up in the bottom of the shower. I quickly got out and opened the door. When I opened the door, water rushed out of the room. Faith yelled and asked as to why the bathroom was flooding. We grabbed towels and began to soak up the water. I prior spent two weeks traveling all over Germany. We visited many old castles, etc., and I did not run into spirits that bothered me. I did not want to alarm my daughter, but I was concerned about my stay at the hotel. During my sleep that evening, I had a vivid dream. In my dream, a little girl kept following me and trying to talk to me. I was at a big party in a large hotel room and everywhere I went, the little girl kept following me. She kept popping out from behind things in the midst of my talking to other people. I was asking her to please leave me alone when suddenly I awakened to my daughter calling my name. When she asked me what was wrong, I could tell her exactly what I said to the little girl. The words were the same in my dream as the ones my daughter heard me saying in my sleep. There was also a man that kept bothering me during the night. Needless to say, I was very glad when we left the hotel.

As I thought about it, I realized I was sensitive to places that have spirits. I remembered an earlier event in my life. When I decided to get a divorce and move to Memphis, I was faced with an apartment with a spirit. A close friend assisted in the search for an apartment home. We moved in during the late afternoon. I was having trouble sleeping and began to unpack boxes while the children slept. I kept hearing sounds coming from the apartment above me. It sounded like someone was dragging something across the floor, especially in an area in the living room. I felt such a 'fear' all during the night. The next morning I decided to go to the office and tell them I needed to get another apartment. We had moved in some furniture, but we had to move. As I walked out the door, I met one of my neighbors. I told the neighbor what happened. She informed me a young man that lived above me had taken his life on my balcony a few weeks prior. The girl living in my apartment was his girlfriend who had broken up with him. Obviously, the apartment manager decided to place me in that apartment due to my living in New York and not knowing the situation. The children and I moved out of the apartment into another building during that day.

During my life, my spiritual experiences were filled with 'love' except for a few leaving a sense of fear. Fear is not something I want to feel and now ask for protection and set boundaries for myself.

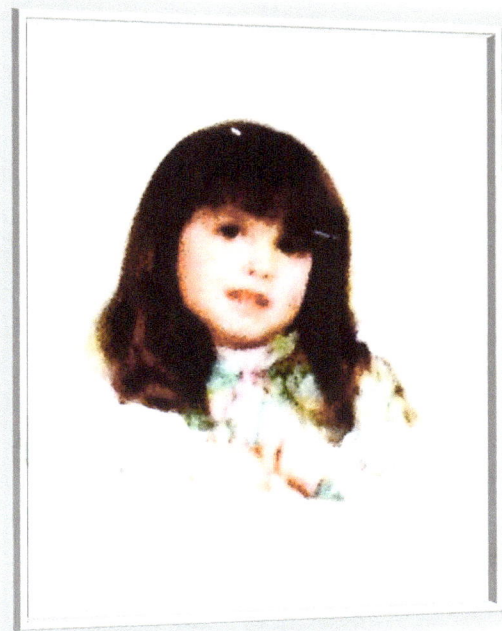

EXPERIENCE #9

BEAUTIFUL PETITE BLACK BEAUTY

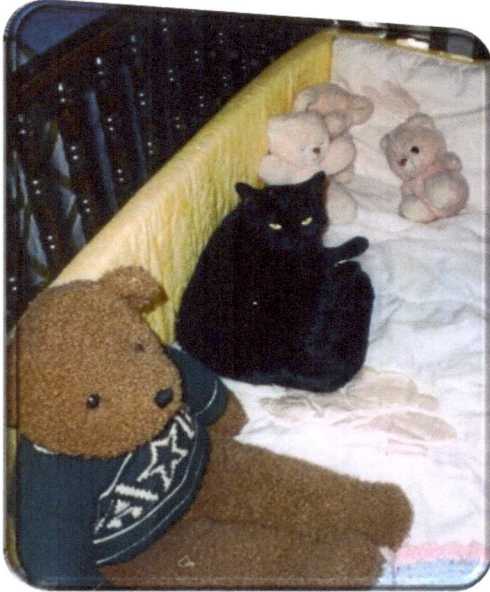

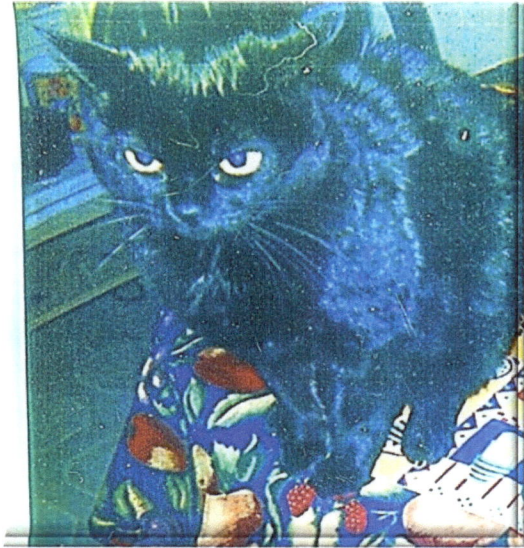

As prior mentioned, Black Beauty was a stray I found at my school. She appeared one cold day crying under my car in the rain. The teachers and students told me she lived at the school for approximately eight months. She stayed in the drain pipes and ate from the school dumpster.

I assume the environment she endured had a detrimental effect on her health. She began to lose weight when she was seven years old. When I took her to a vet, she wanted to run a lot of expensive tests on Black Beauty. I did not have insurance on my animal companions and could not afford the expensive tests. I am grateful insurance is now more affordable for their care in life. Her regular blood test did find she was hyperthyroid and was placed on medication. She lived approximately six more months. The last time I took her to the vet, they recommend euthanasia for she only weighed four and a half pounds. It broke my heart, but I felt I had no choice but to trust the vet's opinion. I did not want her to suffer as I felt Lizzie suffered prior to putting her to sleep.

A few months earlier, I had an important conversation with Black Beauty. I told her I was so sorry she had suffered so much in this earthly life. She stared at me and placed her little right paw on my hand. She left it there a long time as we sat in silence. I knew she understood my message and knew she would be passing soon.

It was only Black Beauty and Zoe left in my life at that time. I would be retiring at the end of the school year and relocate to MS. I moved from my home of nine years to an apartment near my school. Since the apartments would only allow two kitties, my brother and sister-in-law took my other three kitties to find new homes. The apartment was large enough for all my kitties, but my brother reminded me of the rule. They were all beautiful souls that I had taken in as strays in the neighborhood within the past two years. They promised to find them good homes. One, Jake, I will talk about later in the book. The other two Sammy and Cleo went to a nearby town to live with my sister-in-law's brother. I knew their past of neglect and seeking the love of humans and a home. I will always pray for them daily and know I will see them again in our Heaven.

The vet gave Black Beauty the first shot putting her to sleep right away. She soon gave her the second shot and said, "Black Beauty is gone". She gave me a hug for she knew how much I loved Black Beauty. As she was giving me a hug, I heard a sound coming from Black Beauty's body. The vet said it was the air leaving the diaphragm. I informed her I wanted to bury her next to Zoe out in the country. She placed her in a black plastic bag inside her carrier. I called my friend and asked her to meet me at my apartment in order to bury Black Beauty. When I brought her in the apartment, Zoe came out of the bedroom to see her. I took her out of the bag and wrapped her in her blanket. I placed the blanket in a small wood box I had purchased months earlier when I was told she was slowly dying.

As we were leaving the apartment complex, I noticed all the stray cats I tried to feed venturing out and standing by the road as we passed by them in route. I realized they somehow knew I lost my precious kitty in life. It was a rain filled day and only a small amount of daylight left. It was extremely muddy, but we continued to dig a grave for Black Beauty's lifeless body. We placed her next to Lizzie's grave. When we left, we had mud all over us. I found myself ready to retire and losing the ones that gave me 'joy' in life.

I soon had a vivid dream of Black Beauty in which she showed me herself and Lizzie jumping off the coffee table and playing in my living room. I was grateful, for I knew she was okay. A few months later as I was coming home from my night job, I heard a loud meow in my back seat. I stopped the car and went back to see if there was a cat on or near the road. I did not find anything and knew it was Black Beauty reaching out to me in life. One morning Zoe jumped up and walked along my shoulder for a few minutes. I knew somehow it was Black Beauty. Zoe had allowed Black Beauty to use her body to let me know she was still with us in life. Every morning right before I woke up, Black Beauty would jump up on my shoulder and sit until I got up for work.

I am so grateful to God for allowing me to find her under my car on that rainy day and bringing her home. I am so sorry she suffered so much in life and pray she knew how much I will always love her. She was a true Blessing to me in life.

THE BOTTOM LEFT PHOTO IS OF BLACK BEAUTY TAKEN IN MY APARTMENT AFTER SHE PASSED.

EXPERIENCE # 10

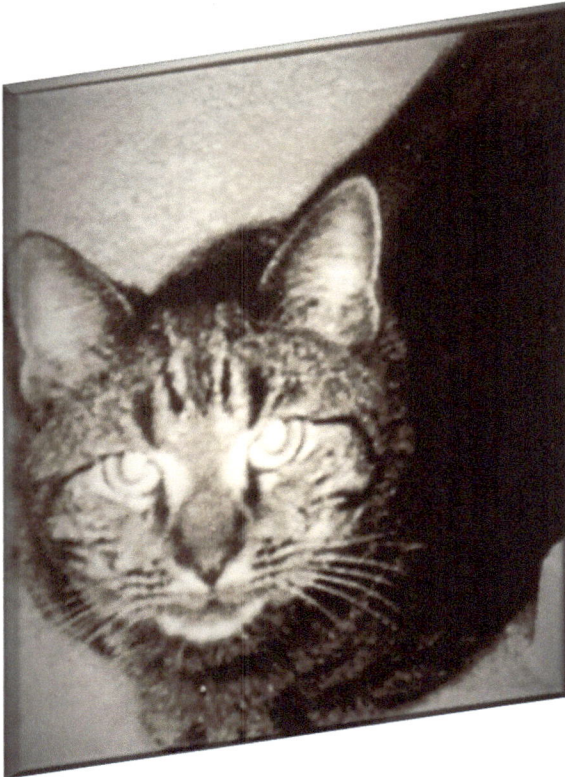

With my youngest child graduating college and moving on with her life, I made a rather quick decision to retire and move back to MS. My brother and sister-in-law assisted in helping me attain and move to a place by a large lake. I felt really lost, for I had worked two jobs for over 16 years in life. I soon found a part time job at a nearby Community College. I was praying I would get to see my three kitties that my brother and sister- in-law had taken back to MS when I left our home. They said I could trust them to find the three cats good homes. Of course I kept Zoe and Black Beauty for they were my first kitties in life. I often think about and pray for all the strays I fed that lived in the woods behind my home in Memphis. I fed one beautiful black cat for nine years. I could see him coming from the woods, jumping the fence twice per day for food. The kitties in that feral colony suffered greatly. Once a friend and I took a very ill one in with feline leukemia and later another with aids. The vet recommended euthanasia, for they would only suffer greatly alone in the woods.

Two of my kitties were living in another town approximately 30 miles away. My sister-in-law's beloved brother gave them a home. Jake was living as a stray in the back yard of a lady in the small town where I was moving. I never understood how he became a stray. It hurt to think of him as a stray again in life. I remembered how scared he was when he lived in a feral colony in the woods. Deep in my soul I felt a fear of him now living so close to the busy main road in town. Jake was only one and a half years old and I feared he would get into that heavy traffic road. I felt he needed to be living inside the house. It was very lonely on the lake, but I was blessed to spend quality time with three of my Aunts in life. I left MS at a very young age and missed out on 'family life' with my relatives. As soon as I moved in, I found a stray dog chasing a rat in a mud puddle in front of my house. Obviously she was hungry and I noticed she was pregnant. She was a gentle soul and I named her Maggie. I decided I would feed her and after she had the puppies, find them all homes. I had a strong feeling Maggie was a victim of abuse. It took a long time for her to raise her head and have eye contact. She would always take part of her food and hide it out by a tree. It is sad to know how so many of these poor animals have to suffer. They are constantly searching for food and water just to survive another day. In Memphis, the problem is so vast, thousands are euthanized yearly after being picked up on the street.

Maggie soon began to sleep on the porch at night. She was always around a male dog named Lake Dog. He was a stray that lived on the lake. In fact, I noticed every night a group of dogs (all strays) came by to get Maggie. They all seemed to like her with her gentle personality.

It was hard living on the lake. The house and grounds were really run down and I was faced with unending work. Unfortunately, that left Zoe alone most of the time. I prior retired from a life of working two jobs for too many years. My life unfolded rushing from job to job. I felt I missed a lot of quality time with my daughter and kitties by working two jobs. My daughter was nine years old when I was forced to leave her alone with the kitties to work my night job. It was the only way I could afford to keep our family unit together in life. I could now tell Zoe was lonely. She would run to the couch at night to sit by me while I was watching TV prior to bed. I remember her daily in the window looking out as I worked in the yard burning brush, etc. Most days were spent outside working on the property when I was not at my part-time teaching job. I am forever grateful to my neighbors that lived directly across the country road on the lake. They lived in a nearby community, but spent part of their time enjoying the lake. They were animal lovers and a real support to me during my stay on the lake.

Maggie soon had seven puppies under my porch. I purchased a large fenced in kennel for she and the puppies. As I drove by the minister's home, I heard my 'inner voice' say, "Why don't you stop by and see Jake?" I slowed down but remembered my brother's words. I said to myself I would honor the loving care of Jake and not bother the minister and his wife with my concern of Jake.

I decided to drive to the grocery store before attempting to put together the large dog kennel. As I was driving down Main Street, I saw a kitty lying in the street. Even though I knew the kitty looked like Jake, I kept driving for a little bit trying to convince myself it was not Jake. I soon pulled over in my Aunt's yard and walked toward the kitty in the street. The kitty's head was face up in the street. It was hard to enter the street, for the amount of trucks and cars on the road. It is a road traveled by a lot of log trucks. The next thing I realized, I was entering a clear tunnel like opening. It seemed as though the kitty and I were all that existed for that moment. As I entered the street, I could only see a haze surrounding me. I did not hear any sounds. As I got closer to the kitty, I initially thought it was not Jake. Something told me to, "Check his collar". I reached down and picked him up wiping the blood from the collar. It read, 'Jake Jacobs'. I held his bloody body close to me and walked out of the street. The cars soon began to move again. My precious Jake, who had depended upon me in life was now gone. He was only a baby and did not have a real home for very long in life. I was crying uncontrollably when I walked over to the porch of the loving preacher's home at which Jake had been living. He asked me if I was sure it was Jake. I showed him Jake and he knew it was him. He, his wife, my sister-in-law and myself shard our cries and love for Jake on that sad day. He took Jake and promised me he would bury him in the back of his yard along with his other kitties.

I lost Jake only six months after I lost Black Beauty. It was a very dark period in my life. I could only think of how I was trying to help Maggie and her puppies and lost Jake. I thought about how disrupted my life had become after making the decision to retire from teaching and move forward in my life. I kept thinking about how young Jake was and how much he wanted a 'forever home'. I watched the older black cat bring him as a kitten out of the woods to my home. He often brought kittens to either my home or my great friend, Jamie, who lived across the street in our neighborhood. We both had a love of animals and this feral cat somehow knew it. He would always stay at a distance watching but he never got closer than his food dish when nobody was around. I often found homes for some, but the nearby shelters were either always full or kill shelters. Jake initially lived out of my garage. He was so grateful for his new home. I often would wake up and look in the garage to make sure he was safely in at night. I eventually moved him into one of my bedrooms trying to get my kitties use to him. He was so happy to finally be inside a home.

When I first heard where he was living, I drove down from Memphis and stopped by the house with my grandson. As we approached the back of the house, he looked up and saw us walking on the driveway. He immediately jumped off the chair he was sitting on and ran up to my grandson. He was so 'happy' and began to jump up and down on my grandson and myself! He followed us to the door of the house. I met the lady and told her I would be back. She said he appeared and was eating from the dish she sets out for all the strays.

I realized the community had a large feral colony. Several older residents left food out for the feral cats. Jake saw us leaving and followed us to the car trying to get into the car. My grandson began to cry and my heart was breaking. We were staying with my brother and my sister-in-law. When we returned to my brother's home, he reminded me I could not have more than two cats at my apartment. He said Jake now belonged to the lady that was feeding him in life. He did not think I should go back to visit Jake. At that moment, I knew I loved my brother and sister-in-law, but realized they did not understand. They would do anything in the world for anybody and were only trying to help me in life. I, on the other hand, had made a commitment to these kitties to find them a home. I felt if God sends you them to help, you can find a way in life. It is a privilege to share with any of Gods beings in life. The 'joy' of knowing you as a mere human being can make a difference in this world is the 'joy' we will feel in our next life.

We all help daily with whatever God has laid on our hearts to make the difference in this world. It is part of our lesson. God sends us the things we need in order to learn our lessons for our soul growth. I grew up observing my family making a difference in human lives. Obviously, along with human beings, God chose to allow me to learn lessons through his little animal beings he placed along my path in life. Our animal companions are sent to bring us unconditional love and assist us with our needs in life. I truly believe we have contracts with them prior to coming to this earth. They are part of our plan made with God and our angels to learn soul growth. They all seem to have jobs to do for us. I know Zoe was a helper with my anxiety in life. I knew a loving retired preacher and his wife lived next door to where Jake was staying as a stray. They were known to love cats and I began to pray they would notice Jake and allow him to stay in their back yard. God heard my prayers and sent Jake to them.

I now realize unless someone works with and cares for strays, they do not realize the suffering they encounter daily. I watched Sammy, Cleo and Jake survive a life in those woods walking daily house to house meowing for food. Jake had a brother and sister that he would play with occasionally during the day. They never left the woods and only came out to search for food. Jake was the one that Black Cat brought to me to find a home. Now, Jake, Cleo and Sammy were all lost to me.

You feel responsibility towards them like your own children. They offer you unconditional love and ask for so little. The stray population is a huge problem for communities. The humane thing to do is each community make laws and provide taxes for humane no kill shelters and care of the feral colonies within each community. All communities should offer assistance for spay and neuter programs. I send out love and respect to all that spend their lives assisting helpless animals find food, shelter and hopefully one day a 'forever home'. We are all connected in the love of our God for all his beings. I will always feel like I abandoned all three of these cats in this life. I shared my home with them briefly leaving them only to search for another home in life. I know they feel my love and know my 'intent 'was good. Our life on this earth is about learning our lesson in order to help our soul grow.

The lessons I, along with many others, learned from Jake are amazing. In a short time on earth, he was able to touch many lives. I left my home without first making sure Sammy, Cleo and Jake all had good homes. Friends and family members have good intentions and help as much as possible. Ultimately, you and only you are responsible for your decisions. Other people do not know your circumstances or the path you were meant to travel in life.

I learned you only have to go within yourself to find the answers. Learning from these three cat lives enabled me to be able to search and find good homes for Maggie and her puppies. The message of growth through this experience helped me as a parent of grown children. We can only listen and offer guidance in their challenges. We do not know the life or lessons they chose to learn and can't make decisions for them in life. All souls have 'free will'. Your spirit must be free to make all choices in life. Your choices within your lessons lead to your soul growth in life. Hopefully we get it right and do not have to repeat the lessons.

Within days of Jake's passing, I saw him out of my peripheral vision. As I turned my head to look, I saw him running and hopping in the woods behind the house. The woods were close and he was now a larger version of Jake. He was so happy hopping like a rabbit. That night I awoke to a vivid dream of Jake. I saw him up above me in all color with a huge halo of beautiful light surrounding him. I knew at that moment he was safely in our Heaven. I am so grateful he forgave me and loved me enough to let me know he was okay in his new life. I truly look forward to the day I will see all my kitties in our Heaven.   Until then, I will continue to send out love and prayers. I feel it important to always send our love and prayers to our family in Heaven. They are only a 'thought away' and appreciate our prayers.

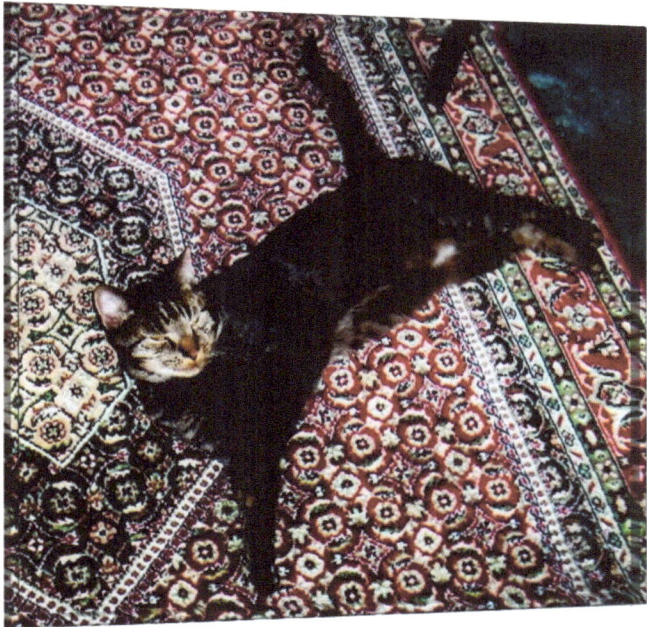

'JOYFUL JAKE'

EXPERIENCE # 11

During my grief over losing Jake, I searched for homes for Maggie and her seven puppies. I found one a home in the local town. The search was hard, for I wanted the puppies to have a good home. It was a long process and I knew I was neglecting my kitty, Zoe. I kept the puppies for six months. In the meantime, Lake Dog, Maggie's best friend on the lake, was brutally killed by a pack of pit bull dogs. Maggie was with Lake Dog when it happened and became very depressed after the incident. I was sitting on the front porch and saw Lake Dog following a man walking along the road a few days before I found out he was passed over. He left the man's side and ran over to the cabins where he stayed mostly in life. He soon got back on the road running to catch up with the man. The next morning a neighbor stopped by to inform me he had been killed by the dogs. Lake Dog was loved by many that knew him on the lake. The neighbor clarified it occurred several days prior to my seeing Lake Dog. I knew he was safe in Heaven.

As earlier noted, life was hard for animals living on the lake. Now, I understand my brother has made a difference in the upkeep of the lake and the lives of the animals living on the lake. I could hear the sounds of nature during the night. I could also hear the coyotes/wolves howling at certain times. I was always in fear of Maggie getting bitten by a water moccasin. Once I was walking across the back yard when I became frozen with an invisible wall. It was the misty clear veil I often see in life. I immediately heard the sound of dry leaves cracking. As I looked down I saw a huge water moccasin as it crossed right by my right foot. I had on flip flops. Thankfully, spirit has helped me at least two other times with an encounter with water moccasins in life. Once a very sad stray dog that lived in the woods of the lake lay dying by my house. I called many people within the county for assistance. Finally, they sent out a person to take the dog to the vet. He was not able to walk. They called me later to inform me he had Rocky Mountain Spotted Fever. I hate to think of how the wild animals must suffer in life. I believe after passing, the wild animals ALL live peacefully in a loving environment in our afterlife. They have helpers to assist them. God sends them to us on earth for our enjoyment and love. It is sad that a lot of humans do not offer them the love they were meant to find in life. As prior noted, the ones that connected and loved humans will spend their eternity with the humans they loved in life. Of course, the animal companion has full free will. Like humans, they have free will to choose to return to earth or to stay in our heaven and learn more soul growth in the realms.

I was blessed to have the love and support of my cousin, her husband, and daughter. They lived several hours away but we talked by phone daily. Later, they took one of the puppies, Meghan, to care for her at their home. They also gave a home to a little stray kitten, Cadee, I found living in the woods along the lake. After many attempts, we finally found a wonderful organization, Homeward Bound, through the Veterinary School at Mississippi State University. I was referred to it by the Humane Society located in a nearby city. My sister in law assisted in getting all the puppies to the vet for their exam, shots, medications, etc., prior to leaving for their new home. A few months later my cousin, her husband and daughter assisted me in getting the puppies onto a bus for a 30 hour ride to a humane shelter in New York. It was sad to separate Maggie from the puppies, but I was assured they were going to a no kill shelter and be placed in good forever homes. I called and checked on the puppies daily until all were place in homes. I will forever pray for them in life.

The organization found Maggie a shelter home in New Hampshire. It was a very sad day when she left. I cared for this suffering, beautiful dog for seven months. I really loved her, especially her gentle spirit. The morning we left, she tucked her tail between her legs as she walked to the car. As we drove around the lake, she stood up and looked at the lake from the window. I knew she realized she would not see the lake again in this life. She was very scared when they took her away to place her in the kennel for the 30 hour bus ride. I called the shelter after the long journey to check on Maggie. They said she was sitting in the office with one of the workers. Due to Maggie being a stray, she needed to be trained to go for walks with a leash. They noticed how gentle she was and promised to find her a good home. When I called the next week, Maggie had a 'forever home'. A prominent lady in the community walked in to look for a dog. Her dog of 14 years had passed and she felt ready to love another animal companion. The shelter manager said as soon as Maggie saw her, she ran to her. The lady and her daughter immediately responded in the same manner to Maggie. Maggie is still in her forever home. Her owner (companion) told me it was hard at first for Maggie to learn to live in a house. It took over a year for her to hold her head up and bark for food. I hear from them at least once per year. She lives in a big house with a back yard that backs up to conservation land. She goes for walks daily and even visits the beach. She developed a thick fur coat to make it through the bitter cold winters. She shares her home and love with a kitty. Maggie was always gentle around my Zoe. When she saw Zoe, she would bow and lay down. She did not want to scare Zoe. She is an amazing spirit and deserves all the joy she can find in life. I am grateful Maggie has a loving home in this life.

As prior mentioned, my sister in law's brother gave a home to Sammy and Cleo in a nearby town. He was retired and lived alone. He was a good man and I am sure he provided a good home for the kitties. Unfortunately, later he became ill and passed to our Heaven. I was told during the month he was hospitalized, his sister came by daily to feed Sammy and Cleo. My sister-in-law said his pastor took Sammy and Cleo to find them a home. At that time, Zoe was very ill and I was busy caring for her. After Zoe passed, I tried to find Sammy and Cleo, but could not reach anyone that had any information on them in life. If they did not have a home, I wanted to bring them to live with me. I was told the small church did not have a pastor. The phone was not in service. I called the shelters in the area, but could not get any information. I pray for them daily. I had a vivid dream not long after my search, and saw Sammy's face. I felt he may have passed into our Heaven. Sammy was a really good soul. He loved all my kitties and grandchildren. He was like Maggie, a gentle spirit in life. A lady in the neighborhood I saw daily walking her big dog, asked me to please help Sammy. He roamed the neighborhood meowing outside every home until I began to feed him. He was extremely afraid of storms. I felt something happened to him in a storm. He deserved a wonderful home in this life. I will always remember him as a gentle little spirit. He first came to us as Lizzie was ill and passing. When I brought her home to say good bye from the vet, he walked over and gently rubbed

Lizzie's nose. After Lizzie passed, he immediately took her place at the front door guarding the entrance of the home. I know I will be with Sammy again in life.

I pray daily Sammy and Cleo are together if they are still on this earth. I pray they found their forever home and the love of a human. Cleo began to hang out in my back yard the summer prior to our leaving our home. One day I saw her out on the patio panting in the heat. The temperature was over 100 degrees. I immediately took her into the house and placed her in one of my bedrooms. I asked the neighbor behind me if she was her cat. She said she was her friend's cat. He left her for a few weeks with her, but now did not want her. She said he was coming by to take her to the animal shelter. I knew the shelter well and knew it meant a certain death for Cleo. I watched her suffer alone for many months and tried to find her a home. She always stood outside watching my kitties from the glass door and windows. One night as I opened the back door, she ran into the house and immediately attacked Sammy. Zoe and Lizzie tried to help gentle Sammy. I separated all and took Cleo back onto the patio. I did not realize how much Cleo looked like my Zoe. Hours later, I realized Cleo was still in the house and I had put my Zoe out in the night alone with all the raccoons, etc. Their markings are the same except Cleo has a scar on her chin from a prior fight. Zoe's white on her back surrounds her to the front white underbelly. Cleo's white markings stops on the back with only a small white spot on the neck. I took her immediately outside and found Zoe still standing alone by the back door. She looked very scared. I remembered the big raccoons that came later in the evening in search of food. I also knew we had some bobcats and coyotes in the woods. I was so grateful she was okay. Of course, I realize the strays have to deal with such an environment every night. I was very grateful Zoe was okay and stayed by the door.

I will always grieve the loss of Sammy and Cleo. I pray daily for them whether they are on this earth or in our Heaven. I know we are connected in love and will spend time together again.

'SURVIVOR CLEO'

MAGGIE, LAKE DOG & PUPPIES

GENTLE AND FAITHFUL SAMMY

EXPERIENCE # 12

My son, Cade, asked me if I wanted to move to Jacksonville, FL, for six months to care for his brother-in-law's two dogs. He was in the Navy and would be deployed overseas for six months. He knew I prior lived at Neptune Beach and loved the area. He also knew my dear cousin and her husband still lived at Neptune Beach. I was always close to my cousin and her husband. They were the godparents of my son. I felt it would be good to spend some time with them in life. The year had been very difficult and I decided to move forward in life with Zoe.

Approximately two months prior to leaving MS, I noticed Zoe not looking right out of her eyes. She began to hide and sleep a lot. I was still busy caring for the lake house property and trying to finish up the last few months of the school semester. One night I noticed her circling the litter box. I knew this meant she had a problem with her kidneys. I thought it was an infection. All my kitties suffered from kidney infections. Zoe had one prior to leaving Memphis, but the vet said she did not have one a few months earlier during a regular check- up. I learned a hard lesson, for the vet needed to take a urine culture. It was expensive, but would show an infection. Instead, the vet said due to her age, it was probably her kidneys failing. This was a very hard situation for Zoe. She was very frightened of vets and their offices. She encountered a bad experience during one of her first visits to a vet. An over aggressive technician treated her badly and she never forgot it. She became very frightened to just go in for her yearly check-up. She would get upset just at the smell of the vet's office being on one of the other kitties during their visits. I wondered how she was going to manage the extra care of her kidneys failing. The vet usually gave her something to ease her anxiety prior to check ups and I knew it would now affect her kidneys.

I took her to get a second opinion. He did the regular urine test also and said it was clear. He said Zoe did show dehydration. He showed me how to give her fluids. It took many trials for me to learn how to get the needle in properly and adjust for the right amount of fluids Zoe needed in life. She lost her appetite and thirst. I told him of our upcoming trip to FL and wondered if she would make the trip. He told me she would be okay as long as she was with me. I remembered those words from that day forward in life. Wherever Zoe and I went for as much time as we had, we were always together in life. I prayed to our God and asked for more time with Zoe in life.

A forever friend, Suzanne, drove down from Memphis and helped me move my things to a storage unit in Memphis. I had no idea where Zoe and I would be or go at the end of our six month journey. All I really wanted was to spend my days with my precious little kitty. I was very frightened at the thought of losing my best friend in life. She had been with me through my divorce; children leaving; losing my other kitties; retirement and move to MS. I could not imagine going forward without her in life. I felt sad and guilty for I knew our move took a heavy toll on Zoe. She was very frightened of all the dogs, feral cats, and wild animals at the lake. I could not allow her out on the deck/porch due to all the animals. I spent all my spare time after work caring for the lake property. I neglected my precious kitty and did not notice the first signs of her illness. Now, I found myself on a limited budget with my retirement and worried how I would afford the upcoming required costs of vets and medications. Deep in my soul, I knew we would move forward one day at a time in life.

Zoe turned out to be a great travel buddy. When we arrived in FL and met Marco and Dennis, I decided Zoe and I would stay on the upstairs level. Marco and Dennis were beautiful labs. I knew it would take time for Zoe and the dogs to get comfortable living in the same house. It took me a while to trust big dogs with my beloved kitty. I spent what money I could on an appointment with Dennis and Marco's vet to check Zoe's condition. The blood test revealed renal problem increasing at high levels. The vet increased Zoe's fluid intake daily. Her technician took time to explain and show me how to administer the fluids properly. I was frightened at the idea of Zoe's kidneys failing, but was so grateful for the time shared on our journey in this life.

I soon found myself attached to Marco and Dennis. It was sad to see how much they missed their Dad in life. Dennis had a thyroid problem and allergies. He was really good about taking his medications. They were so friendly and loving. Caring for them was a blessing. I began to notice Zoe venturing out to the top of the staircase to look at the dogs. She seemed to understand before I did that they were gentle and would not harm her in life.

It was great to be back in Jacksonville. I have wonderful memories of my time spent in Jacksonville, FL. My dear cousin and her husband lived at Neptune Beach. I always felt they were more like an aunt and uncle rather than cousins. It was only a 30 minute drive and Zoe and I went to visit several times per week. Unfortunately my cousin's husband had fallen blowing leaves off the roof of his home several weeks prior to our arrival in FL. At first, he was in the hospital. Zoe and I would go to their home and relax in their peaceful back yard. It was a good experience for Zoe. She was able to investigate around the yard and relax on the steps of the deck. This was a good chance to get Zoe out of the small area upstairs in the house. Zoe had spent her life indoors and I was learning how much she loved being outside.

I read about a progressive vet in downtown Jacksonville. His reviews discussed how he saved animals when other vets gave up on them in life. He also did acupuncture and had a supply of herbs. I made an appointment for Zoe. This vet gave me the hope I needed to stay on my journey with Zoe. He cared for Zoe during my time in Jacksonville giving me the faith and tools to journey forward. He saw how stressed she became when entering the facility and took care of her as soon as possible. He explained her condition thoroughly and answered all my questions. I liked the way he made you a partner in your animal companions care and treatment. He was also an instructor at the Vet school and taught acupuncture. I regret leaving Jacksonville after my time was up taking care of Marco and Dennis. I often wish Zoe and I had rented an apartment on the beach and allowed her to live out her days with the care of her vet in Jacksonville.

Our journey to Jacksonville was a good step forward in life. I met a really nice lady living next door during my stay in Jacksonville. She was a good friend to me during our time with Marco and Dennis. My new friend and I spent many days working on the repair and upkeep of the house. We spent many hours enjoying the dogs in the back yard around the pool. I would bring Zoe out in her kennel to enjoy the outdoors. She and her husband had an older beautiful dog named Lucky. Later, Lucky passed a few months prior to Zoe in life. During our stay in Florida, she would bake dog cookies for Lucky and share through the fence with Dennis and Marco. Zoe and I spent many hours watching the ducks in and around the lake behind the house. My friend and I would go to the store and buy food to feed the ducks. A Mother duck had her babies under a bush next to the front door of the home. I learned a hard lesson about 'living out in nature'. The Mother duck was so proud of her babies. She brought them by to see me the afternoon after she left her home by the bush. She seemed to beam with joy. I later noticed the cranes, hawks, and loose dogs along the lake kill her babies one by one. I called the wildlife services, but they said they could not do anything for the crane was endangered. I could see the cranes and hawks dive down and pick up the little ducks in their mouths and fly off with the Mother helpless to assist her baby. One day I found many ducks killed by a neighbor's loose dog, I found one of the Mother ducks severely injured along the trail. We quickly took it to the vet at the local humane society. At first, they thought it would not walk again in life. Days later, they called and said I could get the duck and release it back into the lake.

We decided to place the duck along with the other Mother duck with her three babies in a nearby lake. We took food over daily and soon saw the crane stalking the ducklings at the new lake. The ducks went back to their original home. I called and hired a company that removes wildlife from properties to relocate the ducks to a safe pond. He was able to move the two Mothers, but could not get one of the babies out in the middle of the pond, for it was getting dark. I worried about the baby all night and early the next morning a young boy and I saw the crane pick the baby duck out of the lake and fly away. For some reason, it dropped the duck and the young boy brought his body to me. We tried to make it to the young duck, but the crane was too fast. We buried the baby duck under a palm tree in the front yard. I also saw a Mother duck and her babies accidentally venture from the pond into the neighbor's fenced in yard with the dog that killed the prior ducks. The dog killed the babies by the time I ran to the house trying to get the neighbor to answer the door. God's beings have a hard time making it in life on our earth. They need assistance from humans. I pray more humans will open their hearts to the love and need of all Gods beings.

I passed through a familiar neighborhood driving Zoe downtown to the vet. I realized I was close to where a dear old friend lived. I knew and dated him when I lived in Neptune Beach all those years ago. I sent a note to the old address in hope some of the family still lived at the home. About one month later someone rang the doorbell. An older man stood at the door and asked me if I remembered him. To my surprise, my old friend had received my note and came by for a visit. His son was now living in the family home. Of course, I did not recognize him at first, but it was such fun to see him after all those many years. After meeting Marco and

Dennis, he asked me if I wanted to join him for lunch. It was great learning about how our lives had unfolded along our paths. He not only knew my cousin and her husband, but also met my family in MS. He always seemed to be fond of my Dad. He lived outside Jacksonville on a place with some acreage. He said he remembered how my brother taught him how to drive a tractor. When I last saw him, he was enjoying life along the beach. Now, I was looking at a person loving his life living in a farm like community.

I only saw him once while in Jacksonville for a few hours, but I had a spiritual experience prior to him leaving. When we walked out the front to go to lunch, he stopped and checked a post on the front of the house. He remarked how it needed repair. When he stopped to look at the post, for a brief moment, I saw my Dad instead of my old friend. I know my Dad also would stop and note the repair. My friend displayed the same mannerisms as my Dad. When we returned, he walked me back to the front door and gave me a goodbye hug. At the moment he hugged me, I changed consciousness. I saw a bright white light encircle me. For what seemed like minutes, I seemed to be in a misty fog. I could only see his face through it. I felt as always, total love and peace from this light. There were people surrounding us in this light. Soon, it all disappeared and all was normal again. My friend seemed very 'joyful' and 'happy'. I did not see him again and often wonder what happened to us on that day. I read that the afterlife/heaven has no linear time. I wondered if spirit allowed me to feel a glimpse of time spent with my friend in our past.

The time flew by and before I knew it, Marco and Dennis's dad was returning home. I was so happy for Marco and Dennis. I did not realize how much Zoe and I had enjoyed our time together in Florida. I prior promised my daughter in Memphis I would move back to Memphis. She worked a lot and needed my assistance with my grandchildren. Prior to going to Florida, I planned on moving to Fayetteville, AR, to live close to my son, Cade, his wife and children. I still was unsure of what I really wanted to do with my life or where to live after my retirement. As prior noted, the' peace' I found in those six months with Zoe in Jacksonville was a gift from God. We moved back to Memphis, but did not find a peaceful environment in which to live our lives. I worked a full time job and a part time job always thinking about what I would do when I retired. I realize now I had it all when I was living my life. I was always truly happy being a single Mom, Grandmother, and Mother to my Kitties. Before I knew it, I was retired, the children were gone and my kitties were passing. Zoe loved me enough to stay with me 'a little longer'. The peace we found those six months in Jacksonville will always be a bright spot in my soul.

We found a high rise apartment (10th floor) in Midtown close to my daughter and her family. It was good to see my three grandchildren living in Memphis. I took the grandchildren to the Circus on the Friday after we moved into our apartment. Saturday, my middle finger and hand was throbbing in pain. Ultimately, I had emergency surgery for a staph infection. Somehow, an infection started from a small cut on my hand. It moved inward wrapping around the tendon connecting my middle finger on my left hand. I was in the hospital days away from Zoe. I begged the doctors to release me, for Zoe needed the fluids in order to survive. I learned from that frightful experience how dependent Zoe was on me at this point in our lives. She was frightened of vets and strangers. She would not allow anyone else to assist her with her with her medications and renal food. Due to having to feed Zoe with my swollen hand with stitches, she also developed the staph infection. Unfortunately, I did not know it for a long time.

The apartment had another detrimental effect on our lives. I noticed some small bugs around the large glass doors leading out to the balcony of the high rise apartment. I did not think much of it since I did leave the door open to allow Zoe to go out onto the balcony. I also was aware we had a lot of pigeons roosting on the roof above our apartment balcony. Later, I realized we were both infested by the bugs I saw at the glass door. At the time, I had longer hair and began to feel bumps on my scalp. I also broke out in a rash on my body, especially the legs and arms. I did not put the rash and bites in my scalp together as from the same source. I noticed bites on Zoe and she was scratching a lot. The vet I was using said he did not want her on flea medications for she was in renal failure. I went to an after hour care one night when I awoke with a swollen round ring bite on my scalp. The nurse practitioner confirmed it was an insect bite, but only administered a shampoo. I could not get the proper help due to it being insects. The medical field did not seem to be of assistance to me or Zoe. My primary physician of over 20 years left his practice prior to my retiring. He left in order to work at St Jude. I did not have a new doctor. I tried many doctors informing them of the bug problem prior to the rashes, etc. They saw my anxiety from the situation and recommended anxiety medicine. I caught some of the bugs with insect hangers, etc., but they still only thought it was anxiety. Of course I had anxiety due to the entire situation. I feel very disappointed I could not find the proper care from the effects of the bug infestation in that apartment. I took Zoe to a vet close to the apartments. She began flea medicine and due to the fleas gave Zoe another medicine for tapeworms. I felt like it was a nightmare. I knew the medications were hurting Zoe's kidneys, but had to treat the effects of the insect infestation.

 When my lease was up, we moved to another apartment, but it was very old, close to an alley and insect infected as well. Zoe's health began to really go down. I bought a little pink pet carrier and took her for daily walks. I always felt the high rise apartment might entail some rather mischievous spirits.   I heard unfound noises late at night from the beginning of our stay. An employee at the apartment complex told me it was haunted. With it being old and many residents passing there, I understood the stories from some of the residents might be true. My next door neighbor had to take her cat to the vet for anxiety medication. She said she was told when she moved in that a resident had passed in the apartment. Her cat would stand at the door and meow all day long. I would notice Zoe stopping, looking up and following something across the floor many times during our stay. Maybe it was just a case of bad luck, but after a hospital stay, infection for Zoe, and a bug infestation, it seemed a lot happening during our residency. I learned to appreciate a safe home in life. I decided to find an apartment near our old home. I understood living on a tight budget and enduring the wait to be able to find a safe home. I walked that path many times in life as a single parent. Walking my path, one of my greatest fears was finding myself and my family homeless.

 We finally found a nice apartment back in the Cordova area to live. Zoe and I continued our daily walks. Our new home was in more of country environment. I had a beautiful view from my upstairs window of nature. We could hear all the sounds of nature on our walks. There were snakes in the area and we had to be careful on our walks. It was hard to watch Zoe's health fail, but I decided to enjoy each moment I had left with her in life. My children and grandchildren continued to come for visits. Zoe spent more and more time in her little bed on my bed. I really missed having the trust and advice from her vet in Jacksonville. The vet in Memphis mostly was there to administer her medications. It was Zoe and I spending what little time we had left in life together. I felt truly blessed to just sit on my bed and know she was right there next to me.

    Approximately two weeks prior to Zoe's passing, I noticed her stomach looking swollen. For weeks, she was continuing to lose weight and become frail in life. I continued to take her out for strolls, but she began to not be able to hold her head up as often and enjoy the view. As I for getting ready to force feed her renal food, she stared intently into my eyes which seemed to be a long time. I heard her message of being tired of being force fed in life. I broke away from the stare, but knew her time was near. That afternoon I became so tired I had to lay on the bed. When I closed my eyes, I saw a vision of Zoe above me telling me she had to leave me in life. A week prior when she was very ill from throwing up and diarrhea, I attempted to give her fluids prior to our vet visit. For the first time, she turned her head around, looking at me and shock her head. I knew she was asking me not to give her any more fluids. The signs were all there, but I was having a hard time accepting them and letting her go. I took her in again to the vet for her swollen stomach. The vet said it was fluid. She said her protein level was so low that fluids was being thrown out into her stomach area. I did not understand, for I had force fed her all this time that horrid renal food trying to keep the protein level low. As prior noted, I only found one vet along our journey that I trusted with Zoe's condition. Unfortunately, he was in Florida and Zoe and I were on our own in our journey.

The vet I was forced to utilize in Memphis informed me there was nothing more she could do for Zoe. She discussed euthanasia, but I had seen an advertisement about a mobile vet I wanted to inquire coming to our apartment to assist Zoe in passing. Zoe was my first animal companion and I knew she would be my last in this lifetime. My other kitties had joined our family and passed on into our Heaven. I wanted Zoe, who was so frightened of the vet office to pass in my arms in her own home. I asked the vet for something for anxiety in order she would not be so anxious when the mobile vet came to our home.

 Zoe continued to throw up at night when she had to use the litter box and screamed out as she looked at me. I prayed for God to please tell me when to make the call to assist her in passing. I prior called and talked to the mobile vet. Fortunately, she was located out in the county close to our apartments. Two nights later, I awoke at 2 am to a 'loud scream' from Zoe. I checked her and she seemed okay. She got on her little bed and went back to sleep. I knew her time was close. Animals are much more aware of the spirit world than humans. They seem to understand and know when their time is near. I kept praying God would give me strength to help Zoe. The next night, I awoke during the night to another 'loud scream' from Zoe. I got up and put on my clothes. I asked Zoe if she could wait until morning for me to call the vet. If she could not wait, I would take her to the all night vet clinic, but I hated to have her in a place she was frightened to pass to our heaven. She turned and stared at something or someone for a brief moment and came over and began rubbing her head on my leg. Even in all her pain, she wanted to tell me she loved me. She again climbed back into her bed and went to sleep.

 When I woke up the next morning, I found Zoe sitting on the floor by her water bowl. I knew there would be no more waiting, for she was passing into heaven. I quickly called the mobile vet and asked them to come as soon as possible. I called my cousin in MS. She called her Mother and together they began to pray for Zoe's passing into heaven.   I gave Zoe the pill the other vet had given to me for Zoe's anxiety. I really wish I had not given her the pill, for it caused Zoe to go into a seizure. I grabbed her and held her close as I waited for the vet. When the vet arrived, I placed her on the bed and noticed Zoe could not move her back legs. I am so sorry, for I know this caused undue anxiety on Zoe. The reason I gave her the pill for to avoid anxiety. I know Zoe knew my intent and forgave me.

The mobile vet was a very nice lady. She said she had gone through putting her own cat of 20 years to sleep several weeks prior and understood the pain of losing a best friend. She was very calming and I wished I had used her as Zoe's vet for the time we were in Memphis. She asked me to sit on the bed holding Zoe as she quietly walked into the room behind me. I took Zoe in her little bed in my arms and held her as the vet began to administer the first shot. As she stuck Zoe, she quickly turned her head to look at the vet. She immediately passed out. She asked me to place Zoe on the bed, for she needed to put an IV into Zoe's leg. She then asked me to hold Zoe while she administered the medicine into the IV. She said she would run a trial to check the IV. When she started the IV, I heard what I initially thought was Zoe having a heart attack! I said to the vet, "Zoe never had any heart problems, but it just sounded like something broke in her heart area of her chest". It was a loud cracking noise.   Later, I realized, the sound our God blessed me with being able to hear was Zoe's spirit separating from her body. She actually passed into heaven prior to the vet placing the last medicine into her IV. I feel truly blessed being able to share her moment of passing into new life.

 The vet asked me if I wanted them to take Zoe's body to Dixie Memorial to be cremated as I had prior informed them on the phone. I said no, for I wanted to drive her myself. She told me to just sit and hold Zoe and cry as long as I needed. As soon as the vet and her technician left, I placed Zoe on the bed to cover her in her small pink blanket. I noticed a large fly on the nearby window. It upset me, for I knew how haunted Zoe and I had been by all the gnats, fleas, etc. I remembered it probably got in when the vet left the door open to get some equipment out of the mobile van. I sat for at least an hour just holding Zoe and crying. I keep looking at her now dark and sunken eyes. She was now gone from that body. I pondered on how so many people could possibly think animals do not have souls. It was June 11, 2013, and my baby, Zoe, was now in heaven. She had moved upward and now I was left to move forward and upward with my own life. I knew we were still connected and would be reunited as soon as I move across the veil. I made a request to my children to place Zoe's ashes with me in my casket when my physical body will be laid to rest.

The days that followed Zoe's passing were spent in grief. It was hard to stop crying and move forward. The following morning as I sat upon my couch reflecting on Zoe's life, a group of crows landed on the railings by my window. They sat on that railing a long time squawking back and forth to each other. Zoe and I always saw the crows on our daily walk around the apartments by the woods. I knew they were aware Zoe had passed. As I was slowly learning, we are all connected in life. I began to notice a misty smoke like substance coming upward from the ground in the woods across from my apartment. I was on the second floor and had a clear view of the beautiful wooded area directly across the street.

I spent time as I did after each kitty passed, going through my old photos and making photo albums. I will always be grateful for a young woman living in my apartment building for the support she gave me during my grieving. During the prior months, I assisted her with her kitty. Her precious kitty was also enduring renal kidney failure in life. The apartment manager knew of Zoe's renal condition and asked me if I could assist in teaching her how to administer the fluids to her kitty. It was a joy to visit with and assist her cat. She was a beautiful and very friendly. I could see the bond of love between my new friend and her cat. I will always remember how patient her kitty was with us in giving her fluids. I was amazed to recognize the fact that our kitties were the same age and in renal failure. We also moved into the apartment complex during the same month. I took all Zoe's belongings and fluids to her kitty when Zoe passed.

On day 10 after Zoe passed, I experienced my first spiritual visit from her. I awoke to my microwave beeping at 3 am. As I was waking from the noise coming from the kitchen, I saw a little figure of white light just above my body. It was in the shape of a little person in a robe. The white lighted figure was holding a white lighted baton and beaming a powerful light over the room. I knew it was Zoe. I felt a great feeling of 'Love'. I turned and looked to my right as I heard the beeping sound still going off in the kitchen. Lying on the right side of my bed was my other passed over kitties. They were lying in Zoe's old spot and looking towards me. As I sat up to go into the kitchen, all disappeared. I was so elated, for I knew my kitties were all safe and together in our Heaven. As I reflected back on the night experience, I thought my Mother brought the kitties back to see me. It was the night after the large family reunion in MS. I also knew how Mother always uses the electrical equipment to let me know she is with me.

The next day, my neighbor's kitty became very ill. She immediately took her into the vet. They decided to euthanize her in the afternoon. It was very sad, for she passed 10 days after Zoe. Strangely, I felt spirit came to visit me and assist my friend's kitty in transitioning into Heaven. My friend felt Zoe paved the way for her precious kitty. My neighbor's Mother came for a visit and offer her support to her daughter. My friend felt a sense of 'peace' in believing her beloved sister in heaven is now taking care of her kitty. I know spirit places the things we need in our life. I feel my friend and her kitty were placed at the right time in our lives. My heart swelled with pride when I saw her a month later go to the local humane society and adopted two beautiful black kitties. She found a good job in GA, and moved her family forward in life.

The early morning visit from Zoe was only the beginning of my spiritual journey moving me forward in life. I was getting older and felt it was not a good idea to get another animal companion. I did not want to leave another behind in life. I decided to donate monthly to ASPCA and help wherever I found a need. I loved my kitties/ animal companions like my own children, and knew we would be together again.

My youngest daughter, Faith, had a baby boy a few weeks prior to Zoe's passing. I knew he was a great gift for me in life. I went to visit Faith and family for a week in Atlanta. The night I returned, I saw Zoe fully materialize across the room. I turned off the TV and began to stand up from the couch. I looked down and standing by the coffee table was Zoe. She was in full color. I was so excited and yelled, "Zoe! She looked up at me with a shocked stare, for she realized I could see her in life. She immediately turned and ran off evaporating into the air. I felt an immense feeling of 'joy' upon seeing her. I can never explain how wonderful it felt. I was so pleased to see her using her little legs, for when I gave her the anxiety pill prior to passing, she could not move her legs. I am so grateful for spirit allowing me to see Zoe.

Soon afterward, I began to have vivid dreams. The following are a short summary of several of my dream visits. In my first dream visit from Zoe, she explained to me what happened to her through pictures. I first saw her lying flat like she was asleep or passed over. I quickly began to try and awaken her for I felt she was dead. She awakened, stood up and began walking down a path. She showed me what looked like baseboards along a wall with a small circle opening. I was frightened for I saw her go into the little hole. Then I was shown a lot of cats. I saw Jake; he was much larger and very healthy looking. I kept seeing faces of happy and healthy cats. I woke up and realized it was Zoe's way of showing me after she died in this life, she woke up, went through an opening into heaven/afterlife. I loved her explanation of how she entered our heaven.

One night as I was meditating prior to going to sleep, I glanced over to my left side wall and saw an irregular circular opening in the wall and saw Zoe. It was as though God allowed me to see Zoe as she appeared in her new life. She was very big and was busy licking herself. She did not seem to be aware of my being able to see her.

One night I was crying when I went to bed. I was feeling very anxious and felt like I was having a panic attack. As my body began to tighten up, I glanced at the ceiling. Right above me on the ceiling I saw Zoe in full color looking down at me. I immediately fell asleep.

I began to recognize the fact that I was leaving my body at night and going places during my dreams. I remembered I first noticed this happening when Zoe and I lived in that high rise apartment in Memphis. The day I found out an old friend had passed, I had a vivid dream. Earlier in the afternoon, I felt the same feeling of a loving presence touching my soul. That night, I was awakened by a loud and far away sounding voice stating, "It is Barbara". I can only remember first feeling a sense of fear and looking back to make sure Zoe was okay. I only knew I was traveling some place with the spirit. I think we all travel to our heaven in our dreams. Most people are not aware and can't remember. God has allowed me to remember some of my experiences. During the two years that followed Zoe passing, I would wake up suddenly in my sleep. It felt a' big jolt 'and I would spend a few seconds moving my hands and arms. It felt like they had gone to sleep and I was moving trying to get them back to working correctly. This happens to me some now, but it was a regular event during the two years I lived in that apartment building after Zoe passed. I truly believe that swampy, wooded area provided an opening to the other side during my healing.

I found the photos provided in this book on my phone one and half years after Zoe passed. I had a retro photo app on my phone that I had not used in two years. I kept it due to my favorite photo of Zoe being saved on this app. One day I noticed Zoe's photo disappeared from my camera. I looked back at the app to see if I still had it saved. To my surprise and shock, all my old photos were gone and replaced with some new photos. I did not take these photos. I only found them due to the sudden disappearance of Zoe's photo from my camera. All the photos were taken in the months following Zoe's passing. After Zoe passed, I put some photos in frames around my living room. I can see these photos in the photos I found on this phone app. I developed these photos from the app and sent a copy to my photo gallery on my phone. As soon as I retained a copy of these photos, the app disappeared on my phone. I am amazed how spirit arranged for Zoe's photo to disappear in order for me to find the photos taken in my apartment. One of the photos is of me. I wore that sweatshirt a lot on cold days. My face looks like it is covered in a mist and distorted. This may mean a spirit has projected over me. I do not know what that is around my neck. I do not wear jewelry. My cousin said it looks like Zoe's collar depicting we are still connected. A lot of the photos have a bold pink color in areas. Several reflect a large pink coming from my bedroom. Zoe passed in my bedroom. I can see several of my passed over kitties manifesting in these photos. I am so grateful for these photos.

As prior noted, a lot of my spiritual contact has been through electrical means. One night, my granddaughter was visiting. She knew I was missing Zoe. She said she wish she could see Zoe like I did. Suddenly, she pointed for me to look. I turned around and my kitchen light was blinking on and off. I told her, "I think Zoe knows you misses her". Later, when we walked into the bedroom, the lights in the bedroom began to blink on and off. She said," I am scared" and immediately, the lights stopped blinking. I explained to her there was nothing to fear. Zoe was just saying hi to her. For me, wherever I go, if I see the lights blink around me, I know spirit is trying to get my attention for a reason.

One month prior to Zoe's anniversary date, the young woman living in the apartment under me took her young life. I was at home and heard a loud and roaring sound. The apartments were new and still under construction. I thought a dumpster had fallen off a truck. It was around 5 pm. Later in the evening, I heard a lot of noise coming from downstairs. It sounded like a lot of opening and closing of cabinets, etc. During the night, I had one of my vivid dream visits. I saw a young woman with long brown hair sitting down and stroking a beautiful long haired dog. She was stroking the dog over and over and staring into space. She said, "You are hurting yourself by not getting another animal. You need to get a dog". I said, "If I get another animal companion, it would be a cat". I awoke and sat straight up in the bed. I was very confused. The next day, I was busy putting together a photo album project. I felt like there was a presence in the apartment with me. I saw a dark figure walk by me several times out of my peripheral vision. I knew it was not my kitties, for I would notice them on the floor and quickly go past me.

I left the house to pick up my grandchildren at school. When I was driving home, I noticed I was right behind my neighbor's car that lived underneath me. I only knew her by name and saying hi when passing her at the apartments. It was a very busy road and I did not see what happened to the car, for it was not right in front of me when I arrived at the apartments. As I parked my car, I noticed her car was already parked in front of her apartment. I wondered how she was able to get home so far ahead of me in all the heavy traffic. The next morning, I had an appointment to discuss a pre burial policy with a nearby funeral home. Now retired and getting older, I wanted to get some affairs in order for my children. My neighbors across from my apartment upstairs both worked at the funeral home. When I arrived, my neighbor said, "I meant to come by yesterday to make sure you knew our neighbor is gone". I was in shock. I live upstairs and face the woods and can't see what is happening in the parking lot. I had no idea my neighbor was dead. Suddenly, I remembered my dream. I knew the young woman I saw in my dream was my neighbor. She only looked a few years younger. She had taken her little dog in the closet with her to take her life. I asked the apartment manager to relocate me to another building, for I was sensitive to spirits. I was so blessed to see and feel Zoe's spirit in that apartment and prayed she was safely in our heaven.

I moved to another building with the same wooded view. I continued to see the misty smoke in several areas in the woods. My dream visits also continued living at the apartment complex. From the first night Zoe passed, I had felt the mattress bounce from what seemed like a jump onto my bed at night. Finally, one late night as I was getting back into bed after drinking water, I glanced back at my doorway. From the nightlight in the hall, I could see the figures of Zoe and Lizzie strolling through the doorway into my bedroom. A few seconds later, I felt the bounce onto my mattress and I fell into a deep sleep. From that moment on, I knew it was my kitties as they came for visits. Another vivid dream involved my actually 'feeling' the hug from a spirit. I was awakened by someone I recognized and I remember being so happy to see this spirit. It was the first time I felt a spirit touch me and I remembered. It occurred a few days prior to my having a hiatal hernia surgery. The surgery was five hours long. I briefly awoke upon hearing my daughter informing me she was going home to see her children. Upon waking, it felt like my chest was caving in and I could not get my breath. I tried to inform her with a faint cry, "I can't breathe". It had been a long surgery and I was having trouble breathing again on my own. As I looked to the end of my bed, I saw a large figure and a female figure both standing looking at me. I knew it was my angel and my Mother. They were very powerful! Upon glancing at them, I fell back into a deep sleep and did not awaken until the night in my room. I found myself lying in a wet bed with my body shaking and teeth chattering. I could not find the nurse button, for it had fallen onto the floor with the line behind the mattress. I tried to call out for help, but was too weak to be heard. Finally, a nurse came to check on me. I had accidentally pulled out my IV during my recovery and the fluids had drained onto my bed. I know my angel and my Mother woke me up to the danger.

I decided to relocate at the end of my lease. My grandchildren came over the last weekend for a visit. I took some photos of the boys early in the evening. We were gazing at the full moon and the great view of the woods. I took several photos of the boys looking out the window and I was amazed at the reflection on the photos. I took these photos with my camera on my phone. All photos are in the back of the book. I truly feel we are never alone and always surrounded by our loved ones.

Now, I only get a vivid dream when something important is occurring or about to occur in my life. I had a dream visit recently after returning home from back surgery. Naturally, the surgery was hard on me. During that time, my daughter's father-in-law was in a nearby hospital in critical condition. In the dream, I was visiting our many groups of people living within a bright light. It was a loving a peaceful environment. I suddenly saw Zoe lying on a gurney. I grabbed her fearing she was dead. She vanished into ashes and I yelled, "She is gone". I then saw another gurney behind Zoe with a human on it. I yelled out, "please, get the nurse for he needs help". I kept telling everyone there is so much suffering. I do not want to go back to the earth. I do not want to see all the suffering any longer. I was told, "They are trying to help, but they are not doing it the right way". Next, I saw myself riding on a train holding Zoe. I was peacefully petting her in my lap and noticed we were crossing a large body of water. I felt the train was high in the air. I suddenly was walking again with others stopping to visit with groups of people. I saw my ex-husband walk by looking like he did in his early forties. He stopped and I remember telepathically asking him how he was doing. The next thing I realized I was at a large celebration. There were lots of joyful people celebrating a life. I noticed it was a woman with beautiful gray hair sitting in a chair surrounded by a large group of people. She raised her head and looked at me with a beautiful smile on her face. It was my recently passed over and loved Aunt. She told me I would have to go back home due to my grandchildren. I suddenly awoke from my dream visit with my arms very stiff and numb feeling. It took a few seconds to get the feeling back.

During the completion of my book, I partially awoke from either an out of body visit or premonition dream. I remember trying frantically to find my hands. I felt no pain and began to think I probably had a stroke. I felt good and had a sense of moving back and forth. It felt like I was not in my body. I felt I could not move my body. I told myself if this is a stroke, I do not want to live without being able to move my body. I remember sitting up and trying again frantically to move my fingers and hands. It was the strangest feeling, for I felt like I was reaching down into my arm to find my hand and fingers. Finally, I felt myself 'find' my hands and fingers. I began to stretch out my hands and all fingers. I was relieved, but still in a deep state of sleep. I lay back on the bed and fell back into a restful sleep. Needless to say, I was relieved in the morning to know I could move my body and did not suffer a stroke. I must admit, the experience left me rather puzzled. I began to research the topic and found some out of body experiences entail sleep paralysis. I now wonder if that is what I am experiencing when I feel a jolt and for a few minutes feel numb and can't feel my limbs.

The few 'out of body experiences' have occurred during a deep sleep. I often hear a loud buzzing sound in my ears during the day. I believe this sound indicates a change in my vibrations.

In another dream, I was told about an unborn baby needing more pieces to survive. I realized it meant the baby needed more time in the womb. Next, I saw my Mother and others around a table taking care of the baby. I was told it would be okay. I awoke and prayed for the baby in my dream. A few weeks later, my sister-in-law called and asked for prayer for her grandson. Her daughter-in-law had gone into labor a few months before the due date for the baby. Even though I did not know if the baby I saw in my dream was her grandson, I told her about my dream visit and I felt the baby in my dream would be okay. Thank God, even though my great-nephew stayed in the hospital a long time, he was okay and doing well in life. As prior mentioned, I feel my Mother and some of my kitties are my guides in life. We all come to this earth with our own guardian angel and guides.

Recently, I awoke from a deep sleep and grabbed my phone to see the time. As I was placing the phone back on the night table, the phone somehow snapped a photo. When I looked at my camera roll to trash the photo, it was a photo of Zoe. It was a photo of my phone screen in which Zoe's photo is my background for the phone screen. For one thing, I know I did not hit the photo app to take the photo. If I had accidently taken the photo, it would have been a photo of me or something in the room. This has happened to me three times during the past several months. I feel it is Zoe saying hi to me from across the veil.

A woman approached me in a bookstore several weeks after Zoe passed. She stood beside me for a few minutes and said, "I hope you do not think I am crazy, but I have a message for you". She informed me she was a professional medium and 'they' insisted she relay the message. She quickly said, "They asked me to tell you that you do not necessarily need these books. You already know the answers you are seeking. All your answers are within your soul. Your answers are in two places within yourself. She formed her hand into a small fist and touched me on my forehead and my heart. She asked me if I understood". I told her, "I do understand and thank you". The woman walked to the counter to pay for her book and left the store. I have not seen this woman again in life. Deep in my soul, I feel 'they' are my angel and guides that surround me and offer guidance along the path I travel.

MOVING UPWARD AND FORWARD IN LIFE

I live my life more fully now. I notice the little things I often missed before in life. I feel everyone has their own angels and guides along their path in life. It only takes opening up and recognizing the signs they leave for us along our path. I appreciate all the love and guidance. I allow my 'love of nature' to 'share my life'. I get lots of signs from spirit in the form of butterflies, moths, dragonflies, birds, etc. I appreciate my children and grandchildren for the spirits I have loved prior to coming into this life. I look forward every day to finding more answers to my myriad of questions on life and new life. I want to know as much as I can about my soul prior to returning home. My earthly life has been spent searching for truths and I look forward to continuing my learning on my soul's path of growth when I pass into the afterlife (Heaven). It has taken a while to document my spiritual experiences. I have encountered more experiences, for it is a daily part of my life. I felt I needed to write some of them down to pass on to my family members. I also wanted animal lovers to be able to read about my experiences with my 'fur babies' passing into Heaven. I pray more humans open their hearts to the unconditional love and teachings of animals. It really hurts me to see how cruel many humans are to animals. Many times humans do not intentionally hurt the animals. They do not see animals as feeling pain, abandonment, loss; hunger, etc. I pray for more compassion for our animal companions on this earth.   My greatest lesson in life has been the importance of 'Love'. I now consider myself to be more spiritual than religious. I personally feel Jesus is the greatest part of our God that walked among us on this earth. His teachings were full of the importance of love and the afterlife/heaven. He brought us miracles and glimpses of powerful assistance from across the veil. I follow the path he left for us in life and believe he does come back to get his followers upon passing. I respect all religions in this life. I truly feel whatever religion a person follows, he/she will find their afterlife when they pass into new life. I feel having a religious belief will help in transitioning into the afterlife. I do not accept any fear based thoughts upon passing. We will review our earth life for soul growth. I pray everyone will find 'peace' in believing all Gods beings pass to new life upon leaving our worn out physical bodies. The more we open ourselves up to love, the more it raises our consciousness during this lifetime. Lessons of compassion and humility are beneficial in raising our vibrations. I walk along my path daily still seeking more truths from my soul. I am so grateful for all my many blessings in life. I seek continuance in raising my level of vibration as I move forward and upward along my journey.

As prior mentioned in this book, I began to notice the orbs outside my bedroom window during the process of documenting my experiences. I continued to see them nightly until I completed my little book. I felt the one close to my bedroom window was Zoe. I prayed for God to let me know as I took a photo of the orb prior to going to bed one evening. I posted the photo at the beginning of the photo section. You can clearly see it is Zoe.   It is a blessing to realize she is one of my guardian angels. God gave me 'peace' in knowing all my kitties are pursuing their soul growth in our heaven.' I envision them continually 'playing among the stars'!

AS REFLECTED IN THE TITLE, I LOOK FORWARD TO PLAYING AMONG THE
STARS WITH MY KITTIES.

DENNIS, MARCO, DUCKS, & BABY CRANES

'PHOTOS FROM SPIRIT'

THE FOLLOWING PAGES OF PHOTOS ARE THE ONES I FOUND ON MY PHONE ONE YEAR AFTER ZOE'S PASSING.

The photos were taken from inside my apartment during my grieving of Zoe. I know the time span due to recognizing several photos I placed in the living room after Zoe passed. I do not know who took the photos, for it was only myself in the apartment. One of the photos captured me. I assume they were left somehow by 'Spirit'. Spirit managed to use my camera to leave me 'physical proof' of the afterlife. As evident in the photos, there is a lot of pink/purple color reflected around the rooms. The apartment photos reflect a misty, smoke like haze (veil) covering the rooms. I also added some photos I later took in my apartment. I did not realize until later they also revealed spirit activity.

THE PHOTO ON RIGHT IS OF AN ORB I TOOK OUTSIDE MY BEDROOM WINDOW DURING THE WRITING OF MY LITTLE BOOK. I COULD SEE ZOE'S FACE IN THE ORB WHEN I HAD THE PHOTO DEVELOPED. THE DATE WAS 07-2016. I ADDED THE PHOTO ON THE LEFT OF ZOE DURING LIFE.

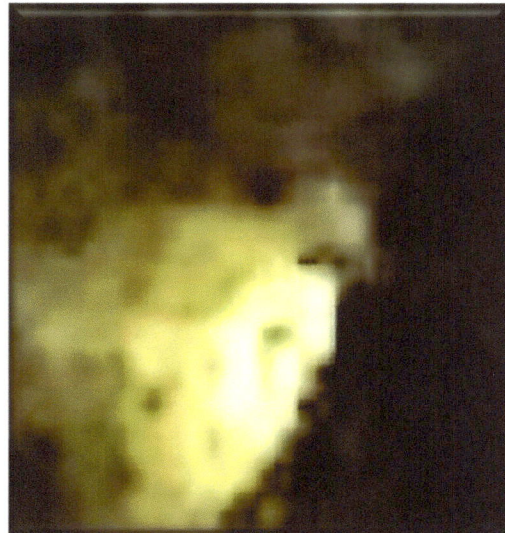

Prior to the writing of my experiences, I sent an email to international afterlife researcher, Victor Zammit, with some of my photos attached. He thought the photos were 'amazing' and recommended my contacting Mark Macy. Mark Macy is a writer and long term researcher in the field of ITC (Instrumental Transcommunication). I sent an email to Mr. Mark Macy with the photos attached. After studying the photos, Mark sent back an email with several comments. Mark replied, ".....You DO seem to have a lot of spirit activity around you....Gabriel in the suit coat in front of the window, the young woman in the woods, all the cats and dogs...wow." I really appreciate Mr. Macy's comments, for it gave me the support I needed to begin my documenting of my spiritual experiences. I referenced several of his comments in the photo section.

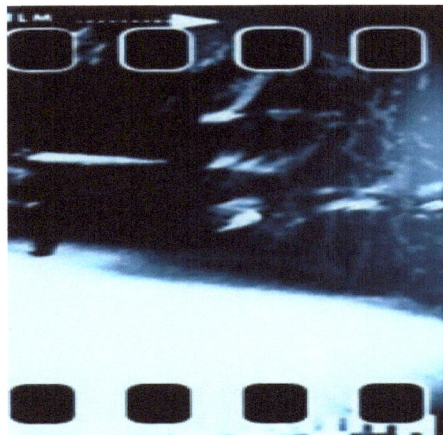

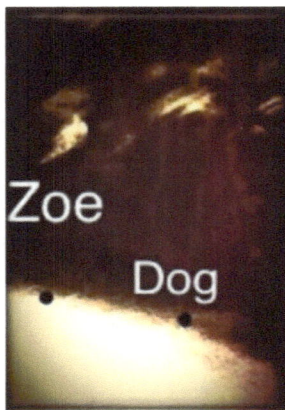

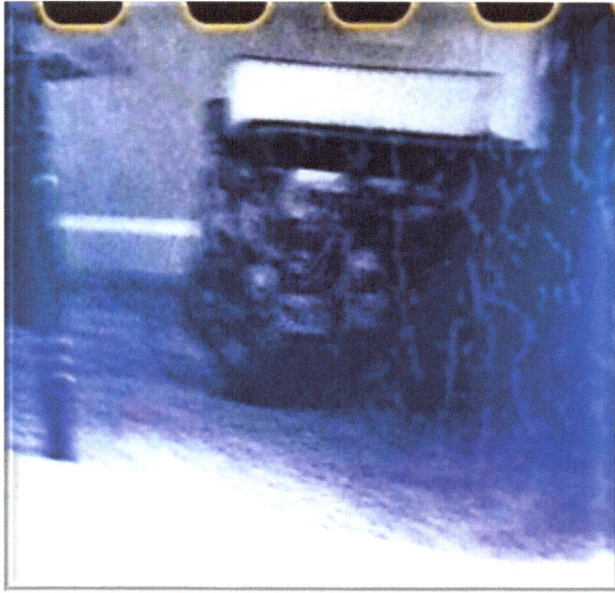

BLACK BEAUTY MANIFESTING OUT OF A PHOTO ALBUM SITTING ON THE FLOOR.

THIS PHOTO DISPLAYS THE SMOKEY, MISTY VEIL THAT SURROUNDS ALL THE ROOMS IN THE APARTMENT. THE MISTY VEIL DISPLAYS IN A PINK/PURPLE COLOR IN MOST OF THE PHOTOS.

THIS PHOTO DISPLAYS ZOE MANIFESTING ON LEFT; A BABY FACE IN MIDDLE BY THE TOP WHOLE IN FILM AND A WOMAN'S FACE OUTLINE ON THE BOTTOM RIGHT FROM BOTTOM OF WHOLE IN FILM TO THE FLOOR.

ZOE IS LYING ON THE TABLE OVER THE PHOTO FRAMES. LIZZIE IS LYING ON THE FLOOR ON THE RIGHT. YOU CAN EASILY SEE ZOE'S MARKINGS ON HER BODY (WHITE FACE WITH GRAY EARS AND PART IN FACE). YOU CAN SEE EYES; YOU CAN EASILY SEE LIZZIE'S DARK BODY ON THE FLOOR ON THE RIGHT; YOU CAN SEE HER EYES AND EARS. YOU CAN SEE THE PINK MIST OVER THE ROOM AND ON THE FLOOR.

I AM WEARING A SWEATSHIRT WALKING ACROSS THE LIVING ROOM.
A HEAVY, MISTY, SMOKEY VEIL IS COVERING THE ROOM.
THERE IS A LOT OF PINK MIST COMING FROM THE BEDROOM WHERE ZOE PASSED.

I questioned Mr. Mark Macy of the ITC about the black 'something' around my neck. He responded, "....I'd assumed you were wearing a black necklace. If not, then maybe there was a spirit with a necklace superimposed over you at the time...In my many spirit face photos, many of the photos had spirit faces totally replacing the face of the person in the picture, and in some of those there was a large collar-like effect...but those never looked as clean and fine as that necklace on your neck." I do not wear any jewelry!

THE TWO PHOTOS ON LEFT DISPLAY A LARGE DARK FIGURE.
THE FIGURE IS TOUCHING THE CEILING.
THE FACE IS MANIFESTING OUT OF THE DARKNESS.

IN THE PHOTO ON THE RIGHT, YOU CAN SEE ZOE'S WHITE FACE, EYES AND EARS PIERCING THROUGH THE SLAT IN CHAIR.
ZOE IS SITTING IN THE WINDOW BEHIND THE CHAIR IN THE LIVING ROOM. I INCLUDED A LARGE VIEW ON BOTTOM RIGHT.

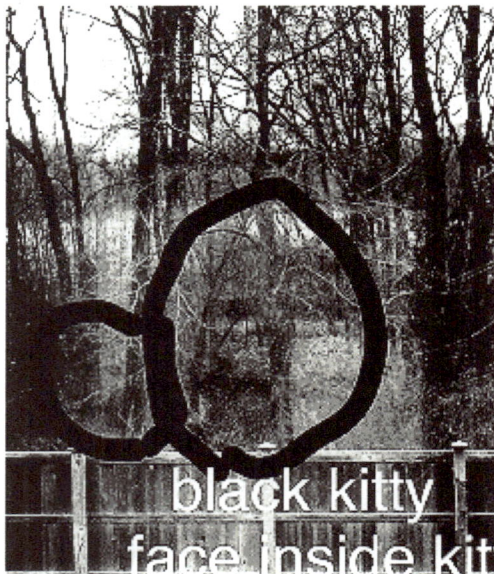

black kitty
face inside kit

THESE ARE PHOTOS OF THE SORTA OPENING I COULD SEE IN THE WOODS ACROSS FROM MY APARTMENT.

Spot I saw Zoe

THIS PHOTO DISPLAYS THE PLACE I SAW ZOE MATERIALIZE IN MY LIVING ROOM. IT LEFT A HEAVY SATURATION OF PINK FROM THE PINK MIST COVERING THE ROOM.

I took the bottom photo trying to capture a bird I saw in the woods. It captures a great figure of a woman materializing on the tree trunk. It also includes an orb to the left reflected on the darker tree. A dark figure appears behind and over the woman. There is a face on tree above figure of woman with a cross above the woman.

Zoe's face orb is on the large dark tree on the left; can see a large dark figure above and over the woman on tree in middle. You can see a face and what looks like a cross above the figure on the tree. You can see other faces in the wooded area.

THIS PHOTO DISPLAYS ZOE'S FACE ON MY GRANDSON'S ARM. A FACE OF A KITTY IS REFLECTED ON THE CHAIR. A KITTY AND FIGURE APPEAR TO BE WALKING ACROSS THE ROOM REFLECTING FROM THE WINDOW.

THIS IS A PHOTO OF ZOE'S FACE IN THE WOODS (orange looking in center).
OTHER KITTY FACES CAN BE SEEN APPEARING IN THE WOODS.

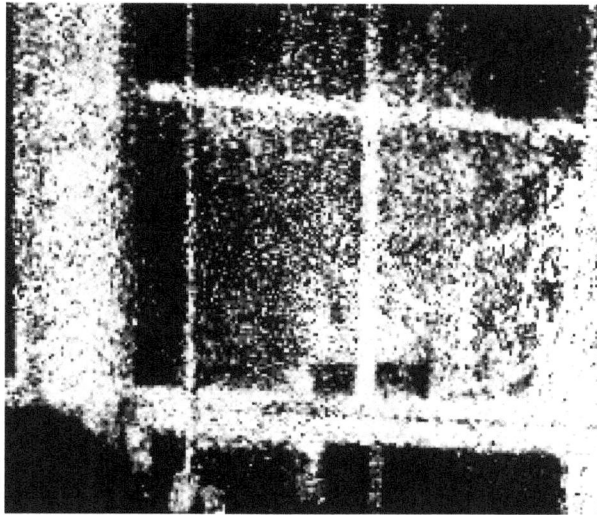

THE TOP PHOTO DISPLAYS A FACE THAT APPEARED IN A PHOTO I TOOK IN MY LIVING ROOM. THE PHOTO NEXT ON THE RIGHT IS OF MY KITTY, LIZZIE, APPEARING IN THE WINDOW PHOTO. MY GRANDSON INFORMED ME HE SAW A BLACK CAT RUN ACROSS MY FLOOR. I SHOWED HIM PHOTOS OF MY TWO BLACK KITTIES AND HE SAID IT WAS LIZZIE. THE BOTTOM PHOTOS DISPLAY A PAIR OF LARGE EYES REFLECTED IN THE LIVING ROOM WINDOW OF THE APARTMENT.

YOU CAN SEE A KITTY'S EARS AND EYES ON BRICK COLUMN IN THIS PHOTO TAKEN FROM MY UPSTAIRS WINDOW. YOU CAN ALSO SEE A KITTY BEHIND THE FIRST KITTY. A DOG WALKER POLE SITS BESIDE THE TREE AND BRICK COLUMN ALONG THE FENCELINE.
ANOTHER KITTY CAN BE SEEN CLOSE BEHIND FIRST KITTY.

I TOOK THIS PHOTO OF MY TWO GRANDSONS THE WEEKEND PRIOR TO RELOCATING. YOU CAN SEE THE FACES OF A MAN AND WOMAN AND TWO MEN IN SUITS CLOSE TO AND IN FRONT OF MY GRANDSON. YOU CAN ALSO SEE MANY OTHER FACES IN THE WINDOW.
(SMALL VERSION)

I WAS WEARING ONLY A WHITE SHORT SLEEVE T-SHIRT WHEN I TOOK THIS PHOTO OF THE GRANDSONS. YOU CAN SEE SOMETHING WRAPPING AROUND MY ARMS AND ANOTHER PAIR OF HANDS. (EXPANDED VERSION)

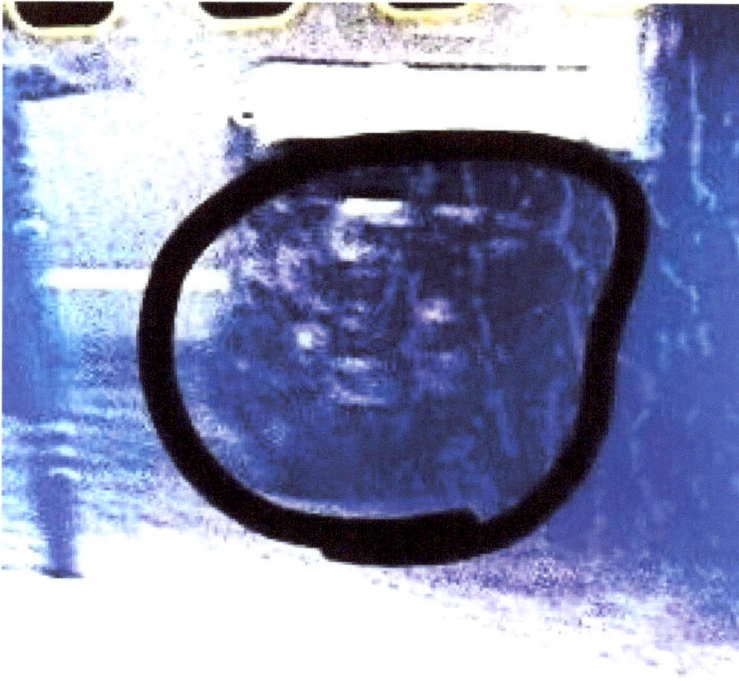

THE TOP PHOTO IS A COLOR PHOTO VIEW OF BLACK BEAUTY AS SHE BEGAN TO MANIFEST IN THE PHOTO. YOU CAN SEE HER EYES, NOSE, MOUTH AND EARS.
I TOOK THE BOTTOM PHOTO ONE EVENING AS IT WAS SNOWING FROM MY WINDOW. I CAPTURED BEAUTIFUL ORBS.

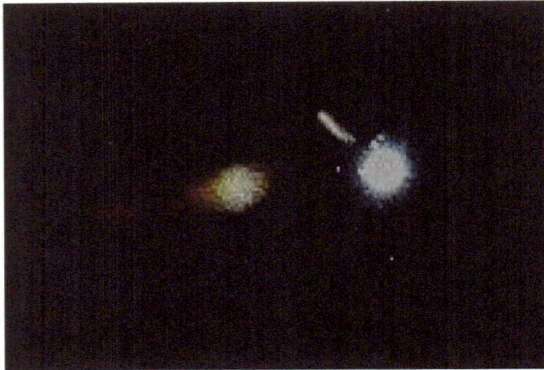

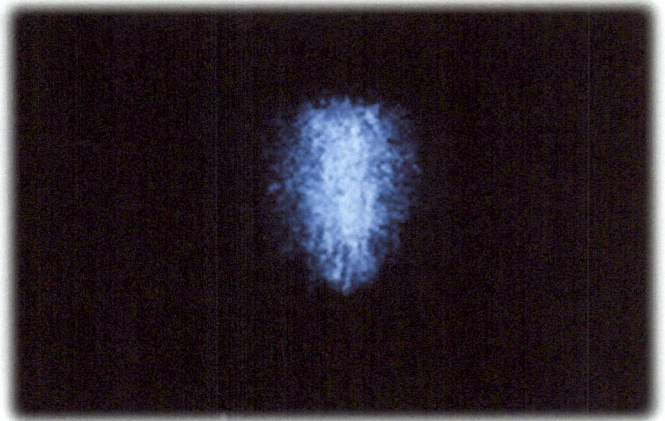

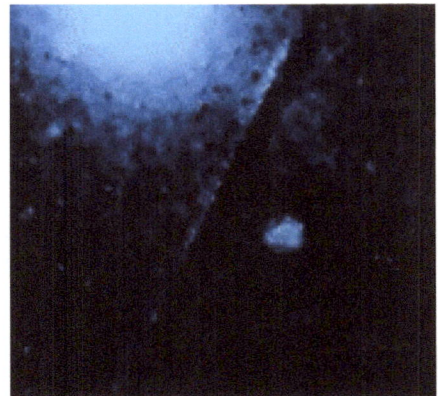

THESE PHOTOS ARE COLOR PHOTOS OF THE ORBS OUTSIDE MY APARTMENT WINDOWS ON 06/21/16.

THIS IS A LARGE COLOR PHOTO OF MYSELF IN THE SPIRIT (SMOKE) FILLED APARTMENT.
(lightened version)

MY DAUGHTER TOOK THE ORB PHOTO IN TOP PHOTO WHILE ON A JOG IN ELMWOOD CEMETERY.   MANY FACES CAN BE SEEN IN THE BOTTOM PHOTO.

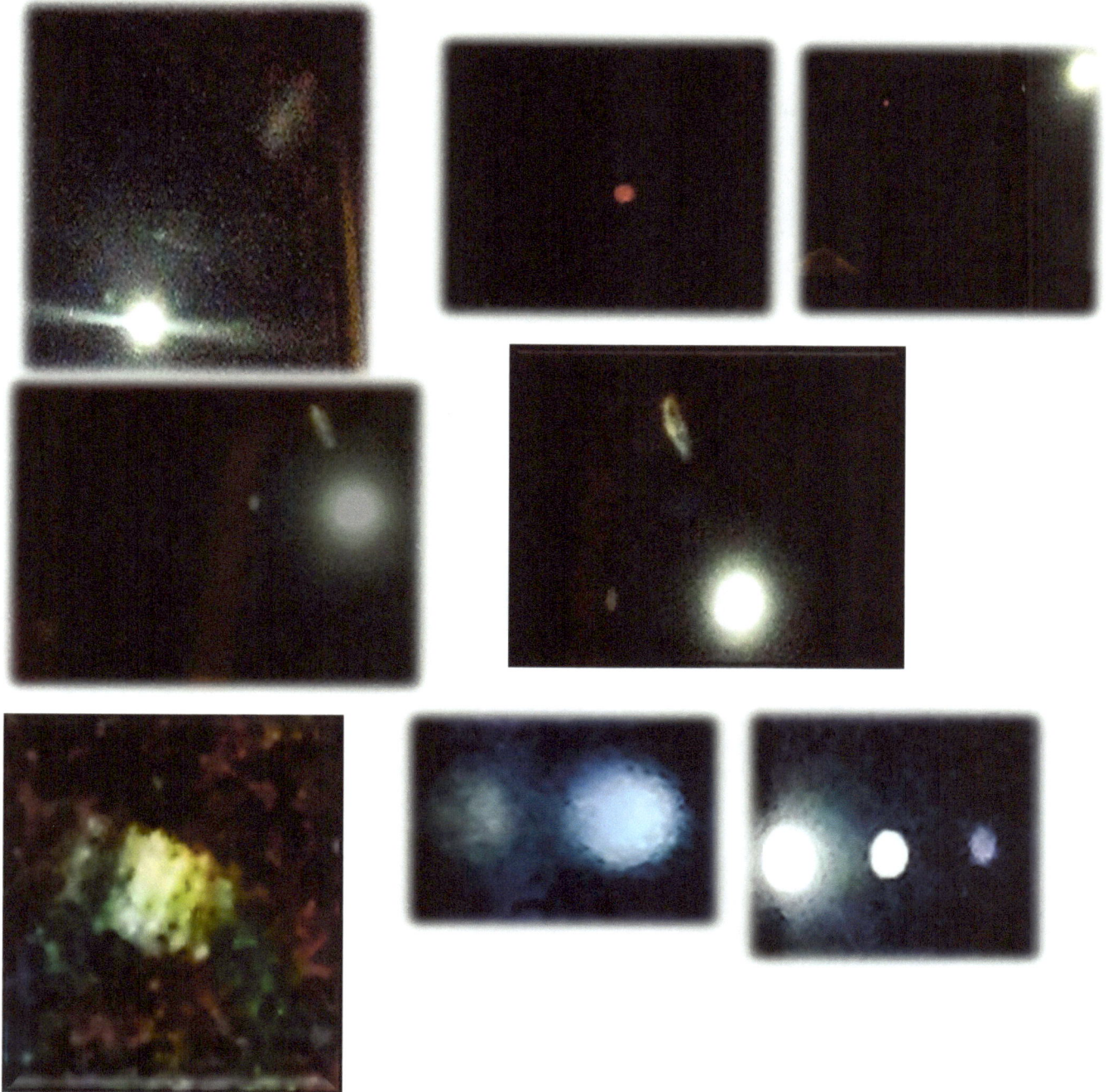

I TOOK THESE PHOTOS ON 07/21/2016. THE LARGE WHITE ONE IS THE MOON. THE ORBS ARE CIRCLING THE MOON. ZOE CAN BE SEEN IN THE ONE OUTSIDE MY BEDROOM WINDOW IN THE BOTTOM PHOTO ON THE LEFT OF THE PAGE.

YOU CAN SEE THE ORBS APPEARING AS ROUND WHITE CIRCLES. YOU CAN SEE THE SHOOTING FIGURE APPEARING OVER THE NEIGHBORS' LIGHT. IT LOOKS LIKE THE SAME FIGURE IN THE OTHER PHOTOS SHOOTING FROM THE MOON. I ALSO SAW THIS FIGURE AT THE TOP OF THE INSIDE OF MY BEDROOM WINDOW.

My Caring Mother

I like her brown eyes.
I like her happy smile
I like the way she talks to me
although sometimes we disagree
on what I eat or where I go but
she always seems to care and
sometimes she's even right about
what I read.
My mother is special to me.
She makes me feel important
when she hugs me.
I watch the way she cares for
other people and hope when I
grow up I'll be just like her.
I remember when my mother
taught me how to read. It
made me feel so happy.

I'm proud of her when she
changes the lives of other
people.
And I like her look of pride
when I get a good grade.
My mother

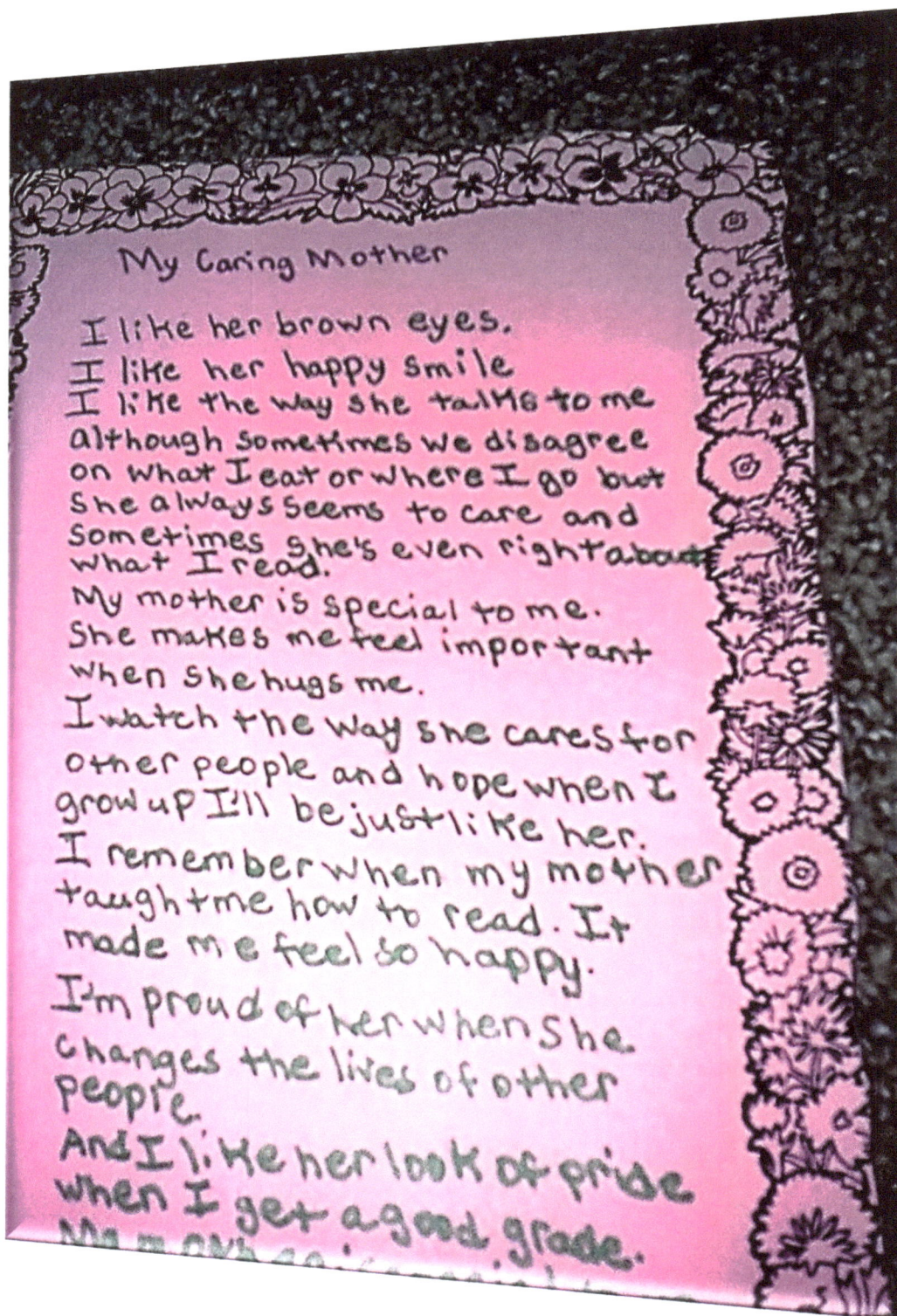

A MESSAGE I FOUND IN MY YOUNGEST DAUGHTER'S ROOM YEARS AFTER SHE GRADUATED COLLEGE AND MOVED AWAY IN LIFE.   'THANK YOU'

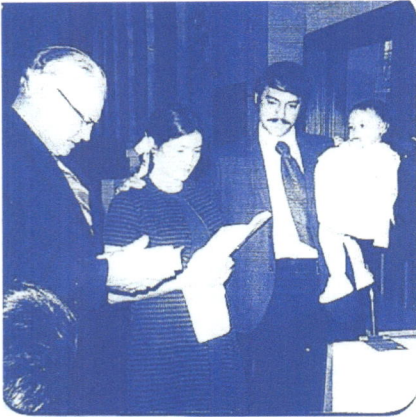

MS JACOBS IN THE CLASSROOM

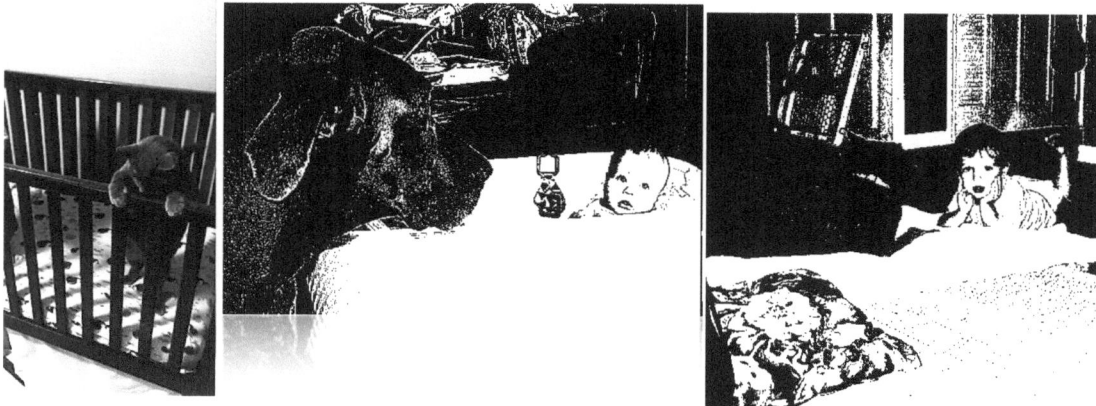

LOVING ALL 'OUR FAMILY' 'FUR BABIES'

ZOE, LIZZIE, BLACK BEAUTY, JAKE, SAMMY, CLEO, SKIPPY

MADISON: TAZ, RAYA; SANDI: CHLOE, TALON,
MAX, SAGE CAT, PHOEBE

CAITLYN AND PETER: MAX, KNEADER, LATTRELL,
SADIE

GABRIEL AND JACOB: NELLIE & ARCHIE

EDWARD AND LUKE: BRUCE
THEY ARE OUR FAMILY AND WE ARE BLESSED TO SHARE THEIR LIVES.

Cadee

'BELOVED TAZ'

WE ARE
ALL

CONNECTED FOREVER

LOVE IS ETERNAL

'Thank you, dear readers, for taking a 'journey along my path of spiritual experiences' in this life.

THE END

ABOUT THE AUTHOR

AUTHOR NAME: ZoeLouise CadeJacobs

-RETIRED HIGH SCHOOL TEACHER
-HOSPICE VOLUNTEER
-MOTHER OF FOUR CHILDREN AND 7 GRANDCHILDREN
-MOTHER TO 6 KITTIES IN HEAVEN
-PROUD VETERAN
I WROTE THIS LITTLE BOOK IN ORDER TO' DOCUMENT' MY SPIRITUAL
EXPERIENCES. MY EXPERIENCES SUPPORT THE BELIEF WE ARE ALL
CONNECTED AND OUR RELATIONSHIP WITH OUR LOVED ONES IS ETERNAL.
I WANTED ALL PET PARENTS TO HAVE THE 'PEACE' OF KNOWING MY
EXPERIENCES INCLUDE OUR RELATIONSIP WITH OUR BELOVED ANIMAL
COMPANIONS. HOPEFULLY, THE PHOTOS OF MY PASSED OVER KITTIES
WILL BE OF A 'COMFORT' TO MANY IN LIFE.
EMAIL ADDRESS: ljacobscade199@gmail.com

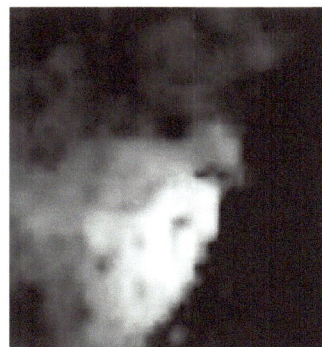